Alternatives to
Social Security

ALTERNATIVES TO SOCIAL SECURITY

An International Inquiry

Edited by
JAMES MIDGLEY
and MICHAEL SHERRADEN

Foreword by
U.S. SENATOR JOHN BREAUX

Auburn House
Westport, Connecticut • London

Library of Congress Cataloging-in-Publication Data

Alternatives to social security : an international inquiry / edited by
  James Midgley and Michael Sherraden ; foreword by U.S. Senator John
  Breaux.
    p. cm.
  Includes bibliographical references and index.
  ISBN 0–86569–245–9 (alk. paper)
  1. Social security—Case studies. I. Midgley, James.
II. Sherraden, Michael W. (Michael Wayne).
HD7091.A48 1997
368.4—DC20   96–41484

British Library Cataloguing in Publication Data is available.

Library of Congress Catalog Card Number: 96–41484
ISBN: 0–86569–245–9

First published in 1997

Auburn House, 88 Post Road West, Westport, CT 06881
An imprint of Greenwood Publishing Group, Inc.

Printed in the United States of America

The paper used in this book complies with the
Permanent Paper Standard issued by the National
Information Standards Organization (Z39.48–1984).

10 9 8 7 6 5 4 3 2 1

Contents

Foreword by John Breaux   vii

Preface   xi

1. *Introduction: Alternatives to Social Security*   1
   James Midgley

2. *The Social Assistance Approach and Retirement Pensions in Australia*   17
   Linda S. Rosenman

3. *Provident Funds and Social Protection: The Case of Singapore*   33
   Michael Sherraden

4. *Noncontributory Pensions in Hong Kong: An Alternative to Social Security?*   61
   K. L. Tang

5. *Privatizing Social Security: Relevance of the Chilean Experience*   75
   Silvia Borzutsky

6. *Pension Reform in Britain: Alternative Modes of Provision*   91
   Matthew Owen and Frank Field

7. *Indigenous Support and Social Security: Lessons from Kenya*   105
    Franz von Benda-Beckmann, Hans Gsänger, and
    James Midgley

8. *Conclusion: Social Security in the Twenty-first Century*   121
    Michael Sherraden

    Index   141

    About the Contributors   151

Foreword

The U.S. Social Security system is undergoing a crisis in confidence. Today millions of young Americans freely express serious doubts that the Social Security system of tomorrow will be able to provide for them in their retirement years. And their concerns are not entirely without foundation.

In 1950, the payroll taxes on sixteen workers were required to provide benefits for one Social Security retiree. Forty years later, only 3.8 taxpayers supported each retiree. Within only fifteen years, as many as 77 million Baby Boomers will begin moving into retirement. By 2013, those retired Baby Boomers may be taking more money from the system than is being collected in FICA (Federal Insurance Contributions Act) taxes. At that point, the Social Security system will begin drawing on its trust funds—buying the system another seventeen or so years. By the middle of the next century, each Social Security recipient will be supported by only two taxpayers—a potentially heavy tax burden for American workers that only forty years ago was spread among eight times as many workers.

Why this dramatic reduction in the tax base for Social Security? The reasons are numerous. Economic growth, so robust in the 1950s and 1960s, has leveled off significantly since the early 1970s. Over the last twenty years, the U.S. economy simply has not performed as well as Social Security's architects believed it would.

The Baby Boomers themselves are largely to blame. While their parents gave birth to record numbers of children in the fifteen years after World War II, the Boomers had far fewer children, providing a shrinking population of workers available to support Social Security when their parents retired. And the demographic trends do not provide much hope for the system's future. If fertility rates decline any further, the ratio of worker to retiree could actually approach one to one.

Whatever the causes of Social Security's woes, almost everyone now agrees that eventually the system will experience a deficit. For years now, we have known that this crisis is approaching. The anticipated Social Security shortfall is not a fiscal tornado that will someday drop from the sky and wreak havoc. It is better compared to a hurricane that we know will someday reach our shores. Unlike the tornado, we have time to prepare. In fact, if we act decisively and soon enough, we even have the power to stave off the fiscal hurricane that threatens our future.

I believe that we can save Social Security from disaster. And I am certain that we do have the resources and the ingenuity to ensure future generations the same kind of financial security in their retirement years that our parents and grandparents now enjoy. But I am also convinced that we can do so *only* if politicians of both political parties quit using Social Security as a political football and begin working together in a bipartisan spirit before it is too late.

At present, there are three major schools of thought in the United States regarding the future of Social Security. The first is what might be called the Band-Aid approach. Proponents of this plan favor raising the retirement age, investing some funds in private markets, bringing state and municipal workers into the system, imposing a small FICA tax increase phased in over several decades, and imposing a slight reduction in benefits. The second approach is more like first aid. Proponents call for raising the retirement age and investing funds in private markets, but they suggest deeper cuts in benefits, including making benefits taxable when they exceed a worker's contributions. The third approach is more like radical surgery. Proponents favor partial or complete privatization, allowing workers to create and contribute to Individual Social Security Retirement Accounts that would divert a percentage of funds from FICA taxes into individual retirement accounts (IRAs).

I believe that the answers to Social Security's woes must go far beyond the "solutions" currently presented by some of our political leaders. Instead, we must look beyond our borders and study the ways that other nations have addressed their social security problems.

Alternatives to Social Security: An International Inquiry is exactly the kind of in-depth examination that national policy makers should study. This important book provides a stimulating and much-needed set of examples of the diverse approaches to social security in such nations as Britain, Singapore, Australia, Chile, Kenya, and Hong Kong. As those of us in policy-making positions grapple with the problem of Social Security and struggle to develop solutions that are equitable for Americans of all ages, the contributors to this volume have given us much to consider. This book is essential reading for anyone serious about addressing the inevitable problems that will face the U.S. Social Security system.

John Breaux
U.S. Senator

Preface

In recent years, concerns about the viability of Social Security in the United States have been raised with growing frequency. Reports on the problems of Social Security now appear regularly. They are derived from studies that show that Social Security, in its current form, may fail to cope with growing demands placed on it by an aging population. These reports have undermined public confidence in the Social Security system, particularly among younger people who increasingly believe that Social Security benefits will have been diminished or even abolished before they retire.

Concerns about Social Security have been exploited on the political Right by policy writers who are opposed to social protections. Managed by the state and governed by principles of collective responsibility, the current Social Security system runs counter to their beliefs in individualism and the primacy of the market. Several reports by right wing think tanks have called for the privatization of Social Security. Other political opponents have been less extreme, most often criticizing Social Security for failing to address the country's changing demographic profile in ways that are fiscally sustainable. Others have challenged Social Security for being administratively wasteful or for damaging the economy.

Amidst all of this criticism, there has been surprisingly little response from moderate or progressive political leaders. Although most politicians privately believe that the Social Security system must be reformed to insure its long-term viability, they remain silent. There is widespread fear, not unfounded, that any serious discussion of Social Security's future will elicit a negative electoral response. Therefore, rather than directly addressing the problems of Social Security, most politicians have avoided the issue. However, as the younger generation becomes increasingly skeptical about future benefits, there will very likely come a time when dominant opinion in the electorate will shift in the other direction, and at that time no politician will be able to remain in office *without* talking about reforming Social Security. This turnabout in the political climate may be approaching faster than we might imagine.

It is time that the issues be debated openly and that a proper analysis of Social Security's deficiencies be undertaken. Perhaps most importantly, this discussion should occur with the cognizance of a rapidly changing economy and labor market as we make the transition from the industrial era to the information era.

The debate on the reform of Social Security should be initiated and led by those who believe in the progressive principles upon which Social Security is based. If progressives fail to assert political and moral responsibility, the future of Social Security will be determined by those who have a different agenda. Progressives should take up this challenge in a manner that is not defensive of the status quo. It is not likely that the solutions of yesterday will be entirely the best solutions for tomorrow. The Social Security system is faced with demands and circumstances that will require innovative responses, including substantial changes in the way that Social Security is funded and operated. As the attack on Social Security becomes more intense, progressive reforms that have a long-lasting impact should be defined and promoted as policy innovations.

In this book we hope to contribute to the emerging debate on Social Security in the United States by drawing on the experiences of countries with alternative policy types. In some cases, alternatives have been introduced quite recently. In other cases, alternative systems have been in place for many years and are regarded as normal and legitimate, although different from conventional approaches in Western welfare states. By examining these alternatives, we hope to provide comparisons that may be useful when policy options are discussed. Policy decisions are more likely to be effective if they are based on careful evaluation of the experiences of other countries. These experiences can provide valuable lessons and directions for constructive change.

As will be seen from the diverse contributions in this book, many countries have based their social protections on approaches different from those used in the United States, where contingencies of old age, death, survivorship, and disability are based on an insurance principle. In this arrangement, taxes levied on wage earners and employers are used to pay benefits to those who meet defined eligibility requirements. Social insurance is used in many other countries as well and is the preferred approach to income protection among international agencies such as the International Labour Office, which has done much to encourage the adoption of social insurance throughout the world.

Despite the widespread use of social insurance, protection can also be provided through alternative policies. In a number of countries, and particularly those of the British Commonwealth, security is provided primarily through compulsory savings programs known as provident funds, which are managed by the government. In still others, such as Chile, compulsory savings programs managed by private firms have been introduced. In still others, such as Australia and South Africa, the social assistance (aid to the needy) method has been dominant. In Hong Kong, a universal social allowance has recently been implemented. Each of these different approaches has strengths and weaknesses, which should be carefully evaluated to determine whether the programs have policy relevance to the United States and potential application in dealing with the challenges facing our nation's Social Security system.

While social policies are often formulated domestically without reference to developments elsewhere, the international transfer of ideas and policy experiences can be of great benefit to policy makers. This book seeks to promote an awareness of developments in social security in other countries so that these examples can inform domestic policy debates and innovations.

We have compiled this book primarily for readers in the United States and other economically advanced Western nations. The purpose of the book is to examine different approaches to social security and to consider whether they offer viable alternatives. We do not suggest that these alternatives can or should be transferred in whole cloth. Nor do we suggest that the current system in the United States, for example, should be totally replaced by the system from some other country. Rather, our intention is to assess international policy currents and explore lessons that can be learned from other countries.

In addition to contributing to policy development, we hope also to promote greater academic and professional discussion of the future of Social Security. The book builds on a companion volume, *Challenges to Social Security: An International Exploration*, edited by James Midgley and Martin Tracy. The primary purpose of the present volume is to transcend an analysis of problems and offer proposals for remedying underlying deficiencies and adapting to changes in the economy.

In preparing this volume, we have received a good deal of assistance from friends and colleagues and we acknowledge their comments and suggestions with gratitude. Especially, we thank all of the authors of the chapters for their important contributions.

James Midgley and Michael Sherraden

1

Introduction: Alternatives to Social Security

James Midgley

Since the end of the nineteenth century, when the first contributory income maintenance programs were introduced in Europe, social security has expanded rapidly and now exists on a worldwide scale. Social security first emerged in Europe in response to pressure to provide social protection to workers in industrial wage employment. Although Germany took the lead, other European countries soon followed and by World War II, social security programs had been established in many parts of the continent. Social security was introduced in the United States in 1935 and has provided income protection for millions of Americans over the last sixty years. Social security programs were also established in some Latin American countries such as Argentina, Chile, and Uruguay in the 1920s and 1930s. After World War II, social security spread to many other developing countries. As these countries achieved independence from European colonial rule, their governments introduced social security schemes for they believed them to be compatible with the need to modernize their societies and emulate the achievements of the West.

The global expansion of social security was accompanied by widespread optimism that the problems of poverty and deprivation would finally be eradicated. Social security programs offered the prospect of providing effective social protection against the risks that reduced, interrupted, or terminated income. In the context of societies where the mass of the population was engaged in wage employment, the contingencies of sickness, old age, death, disability, and unemployment were major causes of poverty. In the United States, the Great Depression had dramatically illustrated the need for a comprehensive safety net to protect workers faced with economic adversity. Social Security promised to maintain income during periods of need, and it is not surprising that it was welcomed by the vast majority of the population. It was generally assumed that Social Security would continue to expand in scope and coverage to protect all citizens against the vagaries of modern life.

Today the optimism that accompanied the introduction of Social Security has waned. Despite the fact that social security offers effective safeguards and has, in fact, reduced the incidence of poverty among old people, the physically disabled, and others, there is growing concern about its ability to provide adequate social protection in the future. This concern is based on predictions that demographic, economic, and fiscal realities will undermine Social Security's ability to cope. Discussions in the media about Social Security's long-term viability have had a negative impact on public confidence, and many younger people now question whether the payments they make into the Social Security system will in fact be available to support them when they themselves retire.

Relatively few politicians have been willing to address these issues. Many believe that to engage in a debate on Social Security is fraught with electoral risks and many prefer to avoid the topic. However, political commentators and social security experts at universities and the nation's think tanks have few reservations about publicizing these issues. Many contend that the system's deficiencies can only be addressed through a major overhaul. Some on the political right have recommended that Social Security be abolished and replaced with alternative systems of care that rely on commercial provisions, family support, or philanthropic endeavor. For them, Social Security is very much on the political agenda. There is an urgent need to fully debate the issues and to determine whether new approaches are needed. In so doing, there is merit in examining the methods of income protection used in other countries. An international perspective can enhance understanding of the problem and offer a sound basis for evaluating policy proposals that may reform the Social Security system and ensure its long-term viability.

FEATURES OF SOCIAL SECURITY

In the United States, the term Social Security is used to connote the federal government's contributory income maintenance program that provides protection against the contingencies of old-age retirement, disability, and death. The last contingency involves the protection of the deceased's dependent survivors. The key feature of Social Security in the United States is the use of the insurance method of funding. This involves the payment of regular, compulsory contributions by employers, employees, and the self-employed. Although these contributions are a tax on earnings and not an insurance premium in the proper sense of the term, payments are based on a contractual understanding that those who contribute to the system while they are employed will receive benefits when they are in need and unable to work.

The use of the term Social Security to describe insurance funded old-age retirement, disability, and survivor's provisions in the United States differs from the way the term is used in many other parts of the world. For example, in Britain, the term is used broadly to refer to a variety of income maintenance programs irrespective of the method used to fund these programs (Hill, 1990). This is not the case in the United States where alternative funding approaches such as social assistance are not known as Social Security. In the United States, social assistance is known as welfare and it is semantically quite distinct from Social Security. In Britain, on the other hand, social assistance is regarded as an integral part of social security. This is the case in many other countries as well (Midgley, 1984; Dixon, 1986).

Although these diverse uses of the term Social Security complicates matters, potential policy reforms of the American Social Security system can be informed by programs in other nations that provide similar benefits even though their administrative and funding approach differs from the contributory system used in the United States. As will be shown in this book, these different approaches have been employed to attain similar social protection goals. However, the extent to which they achieve these goals varies considerably and should be carefully evaluated before attempts are made to adapt these approaches to the United States.

The Evolution of Social Security

The roots of modern-day social security can be traced to charitable activities mandated by religious and cultural beliefs. Almsgiving has existed for thousands of years and it is not only encouraged but required by the world's major religions. The custom of giving charity to the poor is an integral part of Judaism and Christianity, and in Islam the practice is regularized in the form of *zakat*, which is a self-administered poor tax required of every Muslim. Similar provisions exist in Hinduism, Buddhism and other world religions.

While it is historically difficult to draw a distinction between religious duty and secular law, there are many examples of attempts by secular rulers to enforce religious obligations or to organize religious almsgiving through administrative means. One example of this approach was the creation in the seventh century of a public treasury, or *beit-al-mal*, by the Caliph Omar into which *zakat* contributions were paid and then distributed to the needy (Hasan, 1965). Similarly, de Schweinitz (1943) reports that laws were passed by several medieval English monarchs to enforce or modify the religious practice of tithing. Legislation was first enacted in France in 1536 requiring parish churches to register and support the poor, and prior to this, several French cities had established organized systems of poor relief based on the collection of alms (de Schweinitz, 1943). However, perhaps the most important development was the enactment of the Elizabethan Poor Law of 1601, which created a national system of poor relief based on a tax to be collected by the parishes.

The Elizabethan statute is regarded by many observers as a critical development in the historical evolution of social security. It enshrined the principle of state responsibility for poor relief and established a national administrative and fiscal system to ensure that those in need received care. This approach was widely replicated and, in time, became known as social assistance. However, social assistance had several disadvantages. The use of an income (or means) test to determine eligibility stigmatized claimants and fostered their dependence on public benevolence. As eligibility requirements became more stringent, the circumstances of those in need deteriorated and many social reformers began to campaign for the use of alternative methods of income protection, which would guarantee the payment of benefits as of right.

Social insurance emerged as an alternative to social assistance because it established the principle that entitlement to benefit would be earned through the payment of regular contributions. Unlike social assistance, it fostered the accumulation of resources that could be utilized when those in wage employment faced contingencies such as old-age retirement, illness, or disability. The insurance idea originated with mutual aid societies that emerged in the context of nineteenth-century European industrialization to provide a modest degree of income protection to their members. As these societies expanded, the idea that the state should utilize similar methods to offer protection to workers was gradually accepted. The first statutory social insurance schemes were established in Germany by Count Otto von Bismarck, the chancellor, and catered primarily to manual workers. Although the chancellor's intentions were motivated by political rather than altruistic considerations, the working-class movement adopted the idea and campaigned for the introduction of statutory social insurance programs. The German social insurance model was widely copied in Europe and in other parts of the world, including the United States. Another impetus for the spread of social insurance was the adoption of the recommendations of the Beveridge Report in Britain at the end of the World War II (Fraser, 1973). Originally published in 1942, the report is widely credited with facilitating the creation of a comprehensive system of social security, health care, housing, and other social programs in Britain. The introduction of these programs in Britain subsequently facilitated the use of the term *welfare state* to connote the extensive involvement of the government in social welfare. This term was also applied to other European nations where similar programs were created. The report's preference for social insurance also linked the provision of contributory social security with the idea of the welfare state.

The Beveridge Report also recommended the creation of tax-funded, noncontributory benefits for families with children, which would be paid irrespective of income. Known as family allowances, this program was designed to subsidize the cost of raising children. Social allowances have also been used to pay small subsidies to the elderly, those with physical disabilities, and others with special needs. Social allowances are also known as universal or demogrant schemes because they provide income support to particular demographic groups without an income test. However, these programs are not widely used and exist largely in Europe to provide child benefits. As will be shown later in this book, Hong Kong is one of a few non-European territories to operate a social allowance scheme.

Two other forms of social protection should also be mentioned with reference to the historical evolution of social security. The first is the employer liability approach that emerged in the nineteenth century to provide a measure of protection to workers who were injured or killed at work. Originally known as workmen's compensation, this approach placed a statutory obligation on employers to compensate their workers. The employer liability approach was subsequently extended to require employers to provide health care or to maintain wages during periods of sickness and other contingencies.

The second approach is the provident fund that is employed in many Anglophone developing countries to provide old-age retirement, survivors, and disability benefits through compulsory, capitalized savings. This approach differs from social insurance because it does not pool risks and simply returns to workers the amounts they have saved together with accrued interest. Although provident funds have been criticized by many social security experts, they have not been replaced by social insurance schemes as many have recommended. Indeed, they are seen an attractive alternative to social security by a growing number of commentators. As will be shown later in this book, the new Chilean social security system is based largely on the provident fund approach.

Social Security in the United States

As noted earlier, the term Social Security is used in the United States to refer to the federal government's old-age retirement, disability, and survivor's income protection program created by legislation enacted in 1935. Although altered over the years, the programs introduced by the Social Security Act of 1935 have remained largely intact and continue to provide income protection to millions of retired citizens. Originally the legislation only offered old-age retirement and survivor's protection, and it was nearly twenty years later, in 1956, that protection against the contingency of disability was introduced. In 1965, the Johnson administration amended the Social Security Act and introduced health care insurance for elderly and disabled persons. Known as Medicare, this program is often viewed as being separate from the Social Security system even though it is mandated by the same legislation.

The old-age retirement and survivor's component of the Social Security system pays a retirement pension to elderly persons who have been employed or self-employed for a specified period of time and who have paid regular contributions to the system. Currently, qualifying persons are paid a full Social Security pension when they reach the age of sixty-five years. Survivor's benefits are paid to the spouse and dependent children of insured persons who die before they retire. A death or funeral benefit is also paid under certain circumstances. The survivor's benefit is also paid if a retired person has eligible dependents.

Disability insurance provides income benefits to disabled persons who are unable to work because of a severe physical or mental disability. Disability insurance does not provide benefits for illnesses or injuries sustained during employment. Unlike many other countries where employment injury is an integral part of the social insurance system, this contingency is covered under separate programs administered by the states. To qualify for disability insurance, a claimant must have contributed to the Social Security system for a specified period of time and suffer from an injury or illness that precludes regular employment. Eligibility thus requires a full medical assessment of the nature and extent of the disability. Dependents of disabled persons also receive a benefit. Those in receipt of disability benefits may be required to undergo vocational rehabilitation and job placement.

Medicare, or health care insurance, is provided through the Social Security system to retired persons and to those who receive disability insurance. Medicare also provides dialysis services to those with permanent kidney failure. Medicare provides two types of benefits known as Part A and Part B. Part A provides reimbursement for the costs of hospitalization, while Part B provides reimbursement for various other medical services, such as consultation with a physician, diagnostic tests, radiology services, medical supplies, and physical therapy. Reimbursement is subject to limits and may only provide partial reimbursement for actual expenses. Part A Medicare is available automatically to persons receiving retirement pensions, but Part B requires regular monthly contributions as a condition for participation.

Tracy and Ozawa (1995) report that at the end of 1992, some 41 million people in the United States were receiving some type of Social Security benefit. The vast majority of elderly people in the country (approximately 92 percent) receive a retirement pension. Similarly, the great majority of those employed or self-employed were fully covered by Social Security. However, coverage rates for men were higher than those for women; This figure also reflects a lower labor force participation rate among women, as well as the fact that women leave the labor force for periods of time more frequently than men do. Benefit expenditures for retirement and disability benefits amounted to $246 billion or 4.5 percent of gross domestic product (GDP). Medicare expenditures amounted to $107 billion or about two percent of GDP.

These data reveal the extent to which resource transfers currently respond to the needs of retired and disabled people and cater to dependents and those who need medical care. The amounts involved are significant and have, as was noted earlier, been a factor in the emerging debate on the future of Social Security. While some believe that demographic, economic, and fiscal changes will prevent the effective application of Social Security in the future, others point to the critical role these programs have played in preventing poverty. As Tracy and Ozawa (1995) point out, many elderly people would have been destitute had it not been for Social Security. However, the continued efficacy of Social Security in meeting pressing social needs depends on the ability of policy makers to address the challenges currently facing the system.

PROBLEMS OF SOCIAL SECURITY

When proposals for a federal system of social security were first introduced in the United States Congress in the 1930s as a part of President Roosevelt's New Deal, many conservatives vigorously opposed the idea. Many argued that the proposed social security system would have a disastrous impact on traditional values of self-help and personal responsibility and foster an undesirable dependence on government. Some asserted that the social security system amounted to a massive intervention by the state in the private affairs of citizens, imposing a compulsory social program on them and abrogating their right to choose their own forms of social protection. The proposed program, they maintained, would inevitably result in further intrusions by the state, undermine American liberties, and foster totalitarianism. Others were concerned by the constitutional implications of the proposals, contending that the federal government had no right to create national social programs when the constitutional responsibility for these programs rested with the states. This criticism subsequently led to a constitutional struggle in the Supreme Court, which was only resolved after adroit political maneuvering by the president. Others took the view that social security would have a deleterious impact on the economy. The imposition of new social security taxes on a massive scale would, they argued, negatively affect economic growth and exacerbate the serious economic problems facing the nation.

Twenty years after the enactment of the Social Security Act, these criticisms of the program had been largely forgotten. With the exception of
a few uncompromising right wing opponents, most politicians had accepted Social Security as an integral part of American life. The program
had become extremely popular with the public and most recognized that
it made a tangible contribution to the welfare of ordinary citizens. By the
1960s, it appeared that Social Security was here to stay. Many social scientists believed that the institutionalization of Social Security epitomized
an emerging consensus on social and economic issues that would in the
future characterize Western, industrial societies and herald the end of
ideological sectionalism (Bell, 1960).

Today it is clear that Social Security and other social programs are at
the center of a renewed ideological struggle. The rise and electoral success
of the Radical Right has effectively ended the postwar welfare consensus
(Glennerster and Midgley, 1991). Despite the popularity of Social Security
and its documented success in reducing the incidence of poverty among
the elderly, doubts about the system's long-term viability are now expressed regularly. As was noted earlier, concerns about Social Security are
based on predictions that the system will be unable to cope with changing
fiscal, demographic, and economic realities. This has affected public confidence and many ordinary people now accept that Social Security's long-
term future is in doubt.

While much of the rhetoric attending Social Security is ideologically
motivated, there are undeniable problems with the system. Although these
problems have not been addressed in a systematic way by progressive political leaders, they require corrective action. It has already been argued
that temporary corrective measures are an insufficient response and that
more substantive changes to insure social security's long-term viability are
needed.

The Problem of Fiscal Viability

It is often asserted that the American Social Security system is facing a
major fiscal crisis. Although the system is able to meet its current obligations, it will not be able to do so in the future unless current patterns of
revenue and expenditure are modified.

Various predictions about the imminent bankruptcy of the system have
been made. Some experts suggest that Social Security will not be able to
meet its obligations by the end of the first decade of the twenty-first century. Others contend that the fiscal crisis will occur at the end of the 2020s.
These various predictions are made on simple arithmetic assessments of
the point in time at which Social Security expenditures are expected to
exceed revenues. The most respected estimates come from the Board of
Trustees of the Social Security system, which is required to make regular

seventy-five year predictions of the system's fiscal solvency. As Steuerle and Bakija (1994) report, the trustees believe that the system will experience a deficit around 2015. Unless corrected, this deficit will increase further. By 2050, the shortfall is expected to be about 3.7 percent of income. It can be corrected by increasing income, reducing expenditures, or adopting a combination of both measures.

The projected fiscal deficit in the Social Security system is due to various causes. However, it primarily attributable to the way the system is funded. Although insurance funded social security programs in many countries were intended to be financed through actuarially based, accumulated funds, the funded approach as it was known was abandoned and replaced by the pay-as-you-go system by which the contributions of those in employment are used to pay benefits to those who are not economically active. This approach reflected prevailing assumptions about labor force participation, income trends, and the numbers of benefit recipients. It was originally believed that an expanding economy, full employment, rising incomes, and a generally stable proportion of people in retirement would ensure the viability of the pay-as-you-go approach. These assumptions have proven to be incorrect.

It is obvious that the postwar economic trends that promised ever-increasing levels of prosperity were illusory and that recession, inflation, and other economic adversities have had a severe impact on standards of living and levels of employment. The notion of full employment has been abandoned in the Western industrial countries. These changing economic realities have undoubtedly had a deleterious effect on Social Security revenues. In addition, patterns of labor force participation have changed. Self-employment and cyclical patterns of employment and unemployment are now much more common. Similarly, Social Security contributions are no longer based on regular payments by one working spouse. Instead, many more women participate in the labor force than before but many also leave employment for periods of time. Higher rates of divorce have also undermined original assumptions about family structure. In addition, male labor force participation has declined as more men retire earlier. All these factors have negatively affected the anticipated patterns of revenue on which the fiscal viability of Social Security were based.

However, greater demands on the Social Security system for benefits have had a more dramatic effect on its fiscal viability. Demographic changes have had a major impact on Social Security revenues. Original expenditure assumptions were based on stable or declining birth rates and relatively low life expectancies after retirement. Both assumptions have proven to be erroneous. The surge in fertility after World War II resulted in a baby boom that will place higher fiscal demands on the Social Security system in the next few decades. This problem was exacerbated by a decline in fertility in the 1960s, with the result that the ratio of retired to active workers will increase even further. Life expectancy after retirement has also increased dramatically, further aggravating the ratio of retired to active workers. Steuerle and Bakija (1994) reveal that the ratio of those receiving Social Security benefits to those paying contributions has increased significantly since 1950 when there were only six beneficiaries for every one hundred contributors. By 1970 the ratio had increased to twenty-four beneficiaries for every one hundred contributors, and by 1990 it had reached 26 beneficiaries for every 100 contributors. They report that the ratio is expected to increase to 45 beneficiaries for every 100 contributors. The result of these demographic changes is that those who pay Social Security taxes will face greater financial demands to meet the needs of larger number of beneficiaries. Increased contributions to meet these needs may well be resisted, especially if there are efforts simultaneously to reduce benefits. Those who pay Social Security taxes will understandably be reluctant to pay more with the expectation of receiving less when they themselves retire.

These demographic changes raise the issue of intergenerational equity, which has become more topical in recent years. Current calculations reveal that those in retirement now receive more from the Social Security system than they have contributed. This is partly a function of increased life expectancy, but it also reflects the fact that benefit levels have improved since the Social Security system was created. The equity issue is often cited as justification for making fundamental changes to the funding basis of Social Security.

The Problem of Economic Development

Social Security has also come under attack for allegedly impeding economic growth and undermining the nation's economic well-being. It has been asserted that Social Security is a consumption expenditure that detracts from economic growth. It has also been contended that Social Security distorts labor markets and has a negative effect on economic development. Critics of Social Security on economic grounds believe that it should be replaced with alternative forms of provision that contribute to economic progress. However, some economists believe that there is insufficient empirical information to reach final conclusions. Others believe that Social Security's economic impact is neutral or otherwise that it has been positive.

Some economists have argued that Social Security payroll taxes impede job creation and thus harm economic development. In response to high Social Security payroll taxes, employers seek to reduce labor costs and replace workers with machines and labor-saving techniques. Otherwise, they invest in countries where social security and other labor costs are low. These attempts to avoid social security taxes result in a high incidence of unemployment. If employers divest, they transfer capital to other societies and foster their economic development to the detriment of the national economy. Both trends are apparent in the United States and other industrial countries where labor-saving technologies have proliferated and where the problem of capital flight has become more severe in recent years.

Although it is true that both capital export and the use of labor-replacing technology have increased, it is not clear that this is primarily due to high social security taxes. The cost of labor is not only determined by social security taxes but by such factors as the supply of labor, the availability of skilled workers, and wage demands. In addition, the comparative evidence is mixed. Some countries with high social security payroll taxes such as China are attracting foreign investment, while others, particularly in Eastern Europe, are not. Another factor is that employers are likely to consider the cost of labor as a whole when making investment decisions and will still invest if labor costs are comparatively low even though payroll taxes may be high. Labor skill is also an important consideration. Indeed, skilled labor is in considerable demand in many European countries that have relatively high social security taxes. In these countries, social security has not adversely affected economic growth. If this were the case, European countries with lower social security contributions would have performed better than those with higher contribution rates.

Some economists have argued that social security has a negative effect on the economy because it reduces savings and thus reduces the supply of investment capital. This, they assert, retards the rate of economic growth. Social security, it is argued, reduces savings because employees do not save for their retirement, believing that their needs will be met by the government's social security system. The problem is exacerbated by the poor investment performance of social security agencies in countries where reserve funds have been established. A variation of this argument is that social security consumes resources that would, in the absence of statutory schemes, have been invested in commercial insurance. By diverting private savings, social security further detracts from the accumulation of capital needed for development.

Although this argument seems plausible, it is not accepted by all experts. Feldstein (1974; 1977) maintained that Social Security had a negative impact on the savings rate in the United States. On the other hand, a comprehensive study of sixteen OECD countries found no negative effect (Koskela and Viren, 1983). Similarly, as Mesa-Lago (1989) revealed, two studies undertaken in Chile reached opposite conclusions about the allegedly negative impact of social security on capital accumulation. However, Ferrara (1982) has pointed out that even if social security does not reduce savings, a fully funded system that accumulates contributions would significantly increase the savings rate. Social security, he contends, thus involves a major opportunity cost to the economy.

Social security is also said to harm economic growth by fueling inflation and decreasing work incentives. Both factors are believed to be major reasons for economic stagnation. Because social security contributions reduce disposable income, employees constantly demand higher wages, with the result that inflation increases. This trend impedes economic development. A related factor is that social security increases people's expectation that the government will meet their needs. Like other social programs, social security has increased the demands citizens make for government services. The result is a growing public sector, which requires more taxes and bureaucratic intervention, sapping the economy of its vitality. In addition, there is a decline in people's incentives to work hard, save, and be responsible. This further undermines economic development efforts.

The Problem of Managerial Efficiency

Social security has also been attacked on managerial efficiency grounds. Because social security is administered by civil servants, critics argue that it suffers from incompetence, lethargy, and wastage. Like other government programs, its bureaucratic character perpetuates managerial inefficiency. Social security is not subject to the checks and balances of private sector competition. Consequently, those who administer the program have no incentives to be efficient. While managerial incompetence in the private sector would result in bankruptcy, it is protected in the public sector and losses are subsidized by taxpayers. Some critics believe that the costs of managerial inefficiency are enormous and that the problem can only be rectified by transferring managerial responsibility for social security to efficient private providers.

There is little empirical evidence on which to base claims about the inefficiency of the social security administration. International studies have shown that social security programs in some countries are poorly administered and that wastage and incompetence are rife. Mesa-Lago's (1989) research in Latin America is particularly revealing. On the other hand, there are many other countries where social security administrations are highly regarded and where few criticisms of managerial competence have been made. This is not to deny that problems may exist but clearly they are not regarded as a major issue.

Few analyses of the administration of Social Security in the United States have been published. One of the few is Derthick's (1987) account of the decline in staff morale, the rise in internal tension, and the falling levels of productivity within the American Social Security Administration. She reported that the agency had become increasing inefficient in processing claims and dealing with routine tasks. By the mid-1980s, claims took an average of thirty-six days to process, and about 30 percent of claims required more than six weeks to process. Part of the problem was the decline in staff resources following the budget cuts of the early 1980s. But Derthick also blamed other factors, such as inadequate leadership and poor labor relations. She also noted that administrative factors had contributed to errors. A sample survey of Social Security beneficiaries undertaken by the United States General Accounting Office found that payment errors had occurred in 18 percent of cases and that processing, documentation, and other errors had occurred in 32 percent of cases. Derthick (1987) suggested that these errors are costly both to the agency and its beneficiaries and require remedial action.

ALTERNATIVES TO SOCIAL SECURITY: THE CONTRIBUTIONS TO THIS BOOK

It has already been argued that many of the criticisms made of Social Security in the United States are motivated by a strong ideological dislike of Social Security's collectivist principles rather than substantive criticisms of its operations. This belief is substantiated by the fact that many of those who criticize Social Security do not offer remedies that will address problems and improve the system's functioning. Instead, they argue for its abolition and replacement with private modes of provision. As the campaign for privatization gains momentum, the real intentions of Social Security critics becomes more apparent.

Although the ideological nature of the attack on Social Security may inspire an ideologically based defensive response, it is important to recognize that Social Security does face a number of substantive problems that need to be addressed. It is better to recognize the weaknesses of the system than to ignore them under a misguided effort to protect Social Security from criticism. Neither is it acceptable that the status quo be maintained. Despite the fact that many of the criticisms of Social Security exaggerate and sensationalize, those who believe in Social Security should recognize that its long-term viability will be secured through sustainable corrective action rather than denial or minor, short-term reforms.

The following chapters of this book provide accounts of alternative methods of social social security protection used in different countries. These accounts may inform future policy decisions designed to deal with the problems currently facing the American Social Security system. There is value in examining approaches to income protection used in other countries. However, it is not suggested that these approaches should be uncritically replicated. Rather, comparative information can enlighten policy makers and offer a firm basis for evaluating policy proposals to reform Social Security and ensure its long-term survival.

It is important to stress that the following chapters have not been commissioned to address the problems of the American Social Security system. They are essentially case studies of the diverse, alternative approaches to social security being used in other nations. As such, they are self-contained and are significant in their own right. As country case studies, they have been written to promote discussion of the alternative forms of social security currently being used in different parts of the world. Nevertheless, the information provided in each chapter can be easily examined for its relevance to other countries, and its approach can, with appropriate modification, be readily adapted to different situations.

The first case study comes from Australia where social security has been based on the social assistance rather than social insurance approach. Focusing on retirement pensions, Linda Rosenman points out that the system evolved differently from retirement systems in most other industrial nations. Designed to target retirement benefits on needy elderly people, the system is quite extensive, reasonably generous, and free of stigmatizing its beneficiaries as is the case in many other countries. The system also enjoys considerable public support. However, in the 1990s a new compulsory system of private occupational pensions was introduced. Rosenman speculates as to whether this development will undermine and eventually replace the social assistance scheme. She also considers its relevance to other nations. She notes that a recent World Bank report extolled the new Australian two-tiered system of social assistance and private occupational pensions, suggesting that it could serve as a model for other countries. She observes that the current system does have strengths but that it requires the proper integration of the two approaches and a proper recognition of the role of social assistance in a comprehensive social security system.

The second case study comes from Singapore, which adopted a provident fund approach to providing protection against the contingency of old-age retirement, disability, and suvivorship. In later years, the scheme has been expanded to include housing, health care, and other purposes. The Singapore system is based on compulsory contributions and is fully capitalized. Michael Sherraden traces the origin of the system and describes its development and operation in some detail. He also examines its strengths and weaknesses. Finally, he considers its potential adoption in other countries, pointing out that it offers useful lessons for social security policy makers elsewhere.

The third case study describes the noncontributory, demogrant old-age retirement system that has been in use in Hong Kong for over twenty years. The system pays benefits to all persons over the age of seventy years irrespective of income. Like other universal schemes, it is designed to compensate for the costs associated with a particular contingency irrespective of the person's financial ability to meet these costs through his or her own resources. K. L. Tang describes the system and notes that while it pays relatively small benefits, it has helped reduce the incidence of poverty among the elderly. However, while noncontributory social allowances have a role to play, he believes that they should be combined with insurance funded approaches to insure more substantial benefits and more effective social protection.

The next case study describes the new Chilean social security system, which has attracted international attention for being the first major effort to privatize social security. Outlining the history of the privatization, Silvia Borzutzky analyzes its wider political, social, and economic dimensions, pointing out that radical change of this kind is only possible in authoritarian regimes. She describes the workings of the new system and reveals that it is characterized by paradoxes. The costs of privatization have been considerable, its implementation and maintenence require extensive central government intervention, and its staffing requirements have increased. While Borzutzky does not deny that a major reform of the previous system was needed, she does not believe that the new system adequately meets the income protection needs of the population, and she cautions against its replication elsewhere.

In the next case study, Matthew Owen and Frank Field outline proposals for the universalization of private occupational pensions in Britain. Arguing that the country has one of the most extensive systems of private occupational provisions in the world, they propose that all British employees and employers be required to contribute to a system of this kind. However, membership in a private occupational scheme would not involve privatization since it would not obviate the need for a state-managed social security system. Indeed, they insist that a basic social security pension be retained. But to insure adequate coverage for all, they propose that all workers be required to belong to a second tier, private system of income protection. The details of their recommendations, as well as the criticisms that have been leveled against it, are discussed.

The final case study comes from Kenya, a Third World country that, like many other developing nations, has a well-established indigenous system of social support and protection. Noting that there has been growing interest in integrating these indigenous systems with modern, statutory forms of social security, Franz von Benda-Beckmann, Hans Gsänger, and James Midgley review the issue in some detail, using case study material from Kenya to illustrate their arguments. They point out that the industrial countries have much to learn from Third World proposals to utilize indigenous social security systems more effectively. As the industrial countries have institutionalized welfare pluralism and recognized the contribution informal support systems can make to the well-being of their citizens, developments in the Third World need to be monitored and their potential adoption carefully evaluated.

It is hoped that the case studies presented in this book will make a useful contribution to the emerging debate on the future of Social Security. It is hoped that they will provide information about social security approaches in other countries and offer pointers for future corrective action. The case studies are intended to foster the reciprocal, international dissemination of information and aid in the judicious transfer of experiences. In this way, they seek to contribute to the development of appropriate and effective forms of social security that will enhance the welfare of all the world's citizens.

REFERENCES

Bell, D. (1960) *The end of ideology*. New York: Free Press.

de Schweinitz, K. (1943) *England's road to social security*. Philadelphia: University of Pennsylvania Press.

Derthwick, M. (1987) The plight of the Social Security Administration. In *Social security after fifty: Successes and failures*, ed. E.D. Berkowitz. Westport, CT: Greenwood Press, 101–18.

Dixon, J. (1986) *Social security traditions and their global applications*. Belconnen, ACT: International Fellowship for Social and Economic Development.

Feldstein, M. B. (1974) *Social security and private savings*. Cambridge, Mass: Harvard University Institute of Economic Research.

Feldstein, M. B. (1977) Social Security. In *The crisis in social security: Problems and prospects*, ed. M. J. Boskin. San Francisco, Calif.: Institute for Contemporary Studies, 17–30.

Ferrara, P.J. (1982) Social Security: Averting the Crisis. Washington, DC: Cato Institute.

Fraser, D. (1973) *The Evolution of the British welfare state*. London: Macmillan.

Glennerster, H. and Midgley, J., eds. (1991) *The Radical Right and the welfare state*. Savage, MI: Barnes and Noble.

Hasan, N. (1965) *The social security system of India*. New Delhi: Chand.

Hill, M. (1990) *Social security policy in Britain*. Aldershot, England: Edward Elgar.

Koskela, E. and M. Viren (1983) Social security and household savings in an international cross section, *American Economic Review* 73(1): 212–17.

Mesa-Lago, C. (1978) *Social security in Latin America*. Pittsburgh: University of Pittsburgh Press.

Mesa-Lago, C. (1989) *Ascent to bankruptcy: Financing social security in latin america*. Pittsburgh: University of Pittsburgh Press.

Midgley, J. (1984) *Social security, inequality and the Third World*. Chichester, England: Wiley.

Steuerle, C. E. and J. M. Bakija (1994) *Retooling social security for the twenty-first century*. Washington, D.C.: Urban Institute Press.

Tracy, M. and M. Ozawa (1995) Social Security, In *Encyclopedia of social work*, ed. R. Edwards et al. Washington, D.C.: National Association of Social Workers, 2186–95.

2

The Social Assistance Approach and Retirement Pensions in Australia

Linda S. Rosenman

Australia is one of relatively few countries in the world to have modeled its social security system upon a social assistance approach. The system provides means-tested, noncontributory income security to those unable to earn income due to age, sickness, invalidity, unemployment, or sole parenthood. In 1992 the system was modified when the national government created a compulsory national, employer-based contributory retirement incomes system managed by the private rather than the public sector. This development has changed the Australian retirement income system into a three-tiered one comprised of a social assistance base, a national contributory system named the Superannuation Guarantee Charge, and a private contributory superannuation system at the top. Superannuation is the generic term used in Australia to describe contributory retirement incomes programs; they are essentially tax advantaged forms of saving for retirement.

This chapter examines the role of social assistance as an alternative form of social security. It focuses on the old-age retirement component of the Australian social security system. It is important to recognize that the program reflects the history, ideology, and social values of Australian society. Social security programs also mirror the economic orthodoxies of the time, both nationally and internationally. The emergent Australian retirement incomes system has been endorsed by the World Bank as an ideal model for the twenty-first century (James, 1994). However, dominant economic and social theories and views of the appropriate role of the state change over time. It is important, therefore, that retirement incomes systems both promise some stability to individuals while having the flexibility to encompass changes in economic and social values. The Australian system has not been static but has changed and adapted to economic and political changes. Some experts such as Barber (1994) believe that the frequency and extent of change has created uncertainty and threatens to undermine support for the system.

AUSTRALIA: A DEMOGRAPHIC BABY?

In terms of history and demography, Australia is a relatively young society. Australia became a nation in 1901 when the six separate British colonies federated into a single nation, retaining their identity as separate states. Arising from the histories of separate development and as a result of vast geographic distances, Australian states retain separate governments and economic and political powers that affect social and economic development. However, social security, taxation, health care, and other major social welfare programs are federal responsibilities, although the states retain control of the delivery of many social programs.

European settlement commenced in 1788 and, until the end of World War II, Australia was settled by immigrants from northern Europe, predominantly the British Isles and Ireland. It thus retained strong links with Britain and tended to use Britain as a model in many areas of policy, including social security. British traditions were maintained long after they had been abandoned in their country of origin.

Following World War II, Australia embarked upon a planned immigration program to increase its population. High rates of immigration have helped to maintain Australia as a relatively young country, despite very low fertility rates. Currently over 25 percent of Australian residents were born overseas. The majority of postwar immigrants from non-English-speaking countries are now in the ranks of the retired population and are projected to comprise 20 percent of the older population (aged sixty-five and over) by the year 2000. Migration typically disrupts labor force participation and depresses earning capacity over quite a long period. Consequently many migrants have lower earnings and more limited capacities to save for retirement than their Australian born counterparts (Winocur, Rosenman, and Warburton, 1994).

During the twentieth century, Australia has been aging. Currently 12 percent of the country's population of 17.7 million is aged over sixty-five but this is projected to grow to 20 percent by 2031 (Australia, 1992a). Life expectancy has continued to increase and is currently similar to that of most advanced industrial societies. Life expectancy at age sixty-five is, on average, 18.7 years for women and 14.8 years for men. Consequently, the duration of the time that people may have to be supported by the retirement incomes system is a major issue in planning retirement incomes policy.

In addition to extended life expectancy, the length of time that people need to be supported by retirement incomes systems is also closely related to labor market trends. During the last twenty-five years, there has been a steady downward trend in the age of retirement from the paid work force among men. By 1994, less than 45 percent of male workers stayed in the work force until age sixty-five. Although female labor force participation rates have grown, less than 30 percent of women remained in the work force past the age of fifty-five. To some extent this can be attributed to rising real incomes and more generous levels of the Age Pension. But it also relates to labor market restructuring, which has targeted older workers as dispensable.

Australia is an advanced industrial country that has evolved from an agrarian to an industrialized and a postindustrial economy. This has been accompanied by sustained job shedding, particularly in the older manufacturing industries, which has affected older workers. Unemployment rates among older workers have doubled over the past decade and the tendency is to use retirement incomes policy to encourage older workers to leave the labor force permanently.

Australia has always been politically stable. Most political crises have been resolved peacefully and within democratic traditions. Its parliamentary democracy is modeled upon the Westminster system, with two major political parties and a number of smaller special interest parties (such as the greens). The trade unions have considerable economic and political power, particularly during periods when the Labor Party is in government. In 1972, and again in 1983, Australia elected national Labor governments that have operated with a broadly social democratic set of values and with a strongly federalist bias. National social policy has been developed with a strong employment and labor market focus. The Labor government, which has been in power continuously since 1983, has had the political and social support to bring about major structural reforms to social security and retirement incomes policies.

THE AUSTRALIAN SOCIAL SECURITY SYSTEM

The history of social provision for the aged in Australia can be traced to the programs of the states, most of which had introduced some form of old-age assistance prior to or immediately after federation. In 1909, the new federal government took over the old-age assistance programs operated by the states and introduced a national means-tested old-age pension known as the Age Pension. Its main aim was poverty alleviation and the prevention of indigence. Men were eligible to apply for benefits at age sixty-five, but the female eligibility age was set at sixty. Since that time, the Age Pension has remained the basis of the Australian social security system.

Over time, a variety of other noncontributory means-tested pensions and benefits were introduced. They covered those who were unable to work due to sickness (Sickness Benefit), disability (Invalid Pension), responsibility to provide care to dependent children due to single parenthood (Sole Parents Pension), responsibility for caring for others (Carer Pension), and inability to find employment (Unemployment Benefit). Widowhood was also an eligible category until recently when the Widows Pension was phased out, except for those with dependent children. The means testing and structure of benefits for these other categorical schemes has gradually been made similar to that of the Age Pension, although significant differences still exist between the relative social acceptability of the Age Pension and that of the other social security benefits. The entire social security system is funded from general revenues and both policy and administration are the responsibility of the federal government. Receipt of benefits does not require prior contributions or employment history, although legal residence is a requirement for most programs. After categorical eligibility has been established, benefits are related directly to assessed income and assets.

A generous system of health care, disability benefits, and pensions was also introduced for war veterans. Veterans attain eligibility for a retirement pension at age sixty for men and fifty-five for women. This pension (named the Service Pension) is paid at the same level as the Age Pension but effectively allows war veterans to claim a retirement pension five years earlier than the general population. This has had a significant effect on the labor force participation of older men. The majority of those who served during World War II reached service pension eligibility between 1970 and 1985 and many chose, or were pushed, into retiring early.

In 1973, the election of the first Labor government in almost thirty years was based upon an agenda for social reform. This included moving the pension system to a universal basis. In 1973, the means test on the Age Pension was abolished for people aged over seventy, who became entitled to a basic demogrant with a means-tested supplement. The intention was to gradually extend this provision to all age pensioners. A wide-ranging inquiry into poverty in Australia was established which found that age pensioners were among the poorest people in a generally rich country. However, the Labor government only retained power for three years and was not able to introduce all of its social legislation. The Liberal government that followed set about dismantling or reversing most of Labor's social reforms, including the national health insurance system and the demogrant age pension.

The election of a new Labor government in 1983 re-instituted a decade of social democratic type reform, but one that was underpinned by a conservative neoclassical approach to economic management. This approach was popularly labeled economic rationalism (Pusey, 1991). It included a commitment to reduce government involvement in social welfare. As a result of this development, the government's policy was to tighten eligibility criteria in order to target benefits. A review of the social security system was instituted in 1986. Its key aims were to ensure greater equity and adequacy and to integrate social security more closely with the labor market (Cass, 1990).

Over the preceding decade the Australian labor market had changed substantially. Prior to the mid-1970s, Australia had enjoyed a long period of postwar economic growth with low inflation and very low unemployment. Since then a number of major changes have occurred, which have implications for the design and eligibility of social security programs. A major change has been the entry of married women into the labor market. This has changed expectations about a woman's right to be supported by the state if she does not have a husband. Substantial growth in nontraditional employment, particularly part-time and casual work, has also caused a re-examination of the expectations that underpinned the social security system, namely that eligibility for one of the categorical social security programs precludes any form of employment (Cass, 1994).

The Social Security Review recommended a more active linking of labor market and social security programs, with the expectation (despite high rates of unemployment) that reliance upon any form of social security benefit would be a transitional step to employment. The exception to this was the Age Pension. People of pension age were seen as justifiably becoming and remaining outside the labor market. Relatively little attention was given to the relationship between the Age Pension and the labor market position of older people.

Significant changes have occurred in labor force participation patterns at older ages. Since 1970, there has been a marked decline in the labor force participation rates of older men. Male retirement peaks at around age sixty, while women's peaks in their early to mid-fifties. There has also been a marked increase in unemployment rates among older workers. Unemployment rates for men aged over fifty-five doubled in the decade from 1981 to 1991. The incidence of long-term unemployment (unemployed for twelve months or more) has now increased markedly with age (Rosenman, 1994).

The issue for the government has become how to manage this transition between employment, unemployment, and retirement within the existing structure of the social security system. As a result of the Social Security

Review, the unemployment benefit and invalid pension systems have been restructured to encourage rehabilitation, retraining, and active job search. Older workers have been largely excluded from this more active approach. The solution has been to enable unemployed people over fifty-five years of age to obtain an unemployment pension with minimal reporting and job search requirements. This provision is named The Mature Age Allowance. This benefit is effectively a transitional arrangement that gives the older unemployed a pension on similar terms and conditions to the Age Pension.

As in many other countries, concern had been growing since the 1980s about the costs to government of the growing number and proportion of older retired people in the population relative to the population of those of working age. The government believes that one way of reducing future Age Pension expenditures is to encourage alternative forms of saving for retirement that would supplement or replace the Age Pension. As will be seen, this has resulted in the introduction of a national, employer-based superannuation scheme, which the government hopes will play a vital role in the future of Australian social security.

THE SOCIAL ASSISTANCE APPROACH: THE AGE PENSION

The Age Pension is currently the core element of the Australian retirement system and is likely to remain so for the foreseeable future. Accordingly it deserves more extensive discussion as an alternative to social insurance.

The Age Pension is part of an extensive public system of income support that protects people against the risk of loss of income due to retirement, unemployment, illness, disability, or sole parenthood. All of these categorical programs are known in Australia as social security and are administered by the federal government's Department of Social Security. Although some groups are seen as being more "deserving" than others, the Australian social security system has a high degree of public support and the problem of stigmatization is not acute.

In 1978, Age Pension coverage peaked at 78 percent of the relevant age cohorts. Currently, 58 percent of older Australians receive the Age Pension. The proportion of the eligible persons who are pension recipients increases with age. This reflects both the exhaustion of savings and other assets as duration of retirement increases and opportunities of the oldest cohorts to save for retirement during their working lives decreases. A substantial additional number of older people, particularly older men, are recipients of the Veterans Service Pension.

The full rate of pension is fairly low at $8,361 (per annum) for a single pensioner and $13,946 (per annum) for a married couple who are both claimants. A rent allowance is also payable to pensioners who rent in the private market. Although not directly linked, the pension has averaged between 20 and 25 percent of average weekly earnings. Pensions are adjusted twice annually in line with the consumer price index. However, the majority of pensioners do not receive the full rate of pension. This is due to a relatively generous phase out or benefit reduction rate for the pension.

The benefit reduction rate is set at 50 percent after an income test free amount. This allows people to draw a partial pension up to an annual income of $32,219 (per annum) if married and $19,333 (per annum) if single. This effectively means that people can be drawing a partial pension at income levels above those of many income earners in the Australian population who are not pension eligible.

The assessment of income and assets for pension eligibility has been subject to many changes during the past twenty years. During the 1970s, there was a loosening of eligibility criteria with the removal of the assets test. In 1976, the assets test component of the means test was abolished and eligibility was assessed on the basis of an income test only. In 1985, an assets test was re-introduced. However, people can still have fairly considerable assets, including a home and up to $224,000 of other possessions if single and $306,000 if married.

In 1991, the government turned its attention to the savings of pensioners, which were often being kept in accounts with low or no interest in order to minimize assessable income and to maximize pension eligibility. Beyond a very low level of assessed savings, pensioners are deemed by the government to be earning interest (at current market interest rates) on all savings and investments above $2,000. These levels are reviewed regularly to reflect current conditions. Nevertheless, the gradual tightening of eligibility criteria has led to a reduction in the percentage of the older population eligible for the Age Pension.

The pension is paid at either a single or a married rate. Each member of a married couple receives less individually than a single pensioner, which reflects assumptions about economies in sharing of living expenses. Income and assets are assessed on the basis of marital status and cohabitation. Older people who share a home but who are not married (such as siblings) are assessed for and receive the single rate of pension. Until 1995, the spouse of a pension eligible man could become eligible for a Wife's Pension regardless of age simply on the basis of family income and assets. This has been a significant disincentive to continued labor force participation for women married to older men. The income unit for eligibility, assessment, and payment varies between social security pension categories and is not compatible with the taxation system.

The taxation of pension beneficiaries remains a complex topic. Pensioners who receive a part of their income from the pension and part from other income sources have effectively been double-taxed due to the combination of the 50 percent benefit reduction rate and the imposition of income taxation. The government has now committed itself to removing all pensioners from the tax system. This runs the risk of introducing other inequities since some pensioners will be living tax free on income levels that would attract tax for regular income earners. With the growth of superannuation coverage, many retirees are now living on partial age pensions combined with income from superannuation, which has already enjoyed generous tax exemptions on contributions, fund earnings, and benefits (Brown, 1994).

In addition to the tax benefits of receiving the pension, there are significant noncash benefits that accrue to those with pension status. These include exemption from contributions to the national health insurance system and eligibility for exemption from the co-payment for medical treatment. Also included are a generous subsidy on purchases of prescription medications, discounts on telephone rental, public transport, local government taxes, and on a range of other privately provided services such as hairdressers and even entertainment. The value of many of these non-monetary benefits is a significant incentive to pensioners to minimize other income in order to retain eligibility for benefits. On a state-by-state basis, there has been an expansion of some of these benefits to all people of pension age through the awarding of Seniors Cards that entitle them to free services. These cards have helped to reduce but not eliminate some of the incentives for people to establish and maintain pension eligibility that were related to the potential value of in-kind benefits.

The Emergence of Contributory Retirement Programs

A discussion of the viability of social assistance as an alternative form of social security must take into the account fact that there has been extensive discussion in Australia about replacing the social assistance Age Pension with an insurance scheme. Through most of this century, there have been attempts by both the Liberal and Labor governments to introduce a national contributory pensions scheme. In 1938, a contributory pension scheme was proposed and legislated for, but World War II stopped its implementation. In 1945, a special tax levy was introduced to create a National Welfare Fund to pay for social welfare programs. However, since no insurance scheme had been introduced, the monies raised were spent immediately, and the levy ceased five years later. In 1972, the new Labor government proposed the creation of a national superannuation scheme but did not follow it through. In 1977, a commission of inquiry was established to review the issue. It recommended the establishment of a national contributory superannuation scheme. By the time the commission had reported in 1979, the political situation had changed and its recommendation was shelved.

The election of a Labor government in 1983 put socioeconomic reform back on the agenda. The cost to the government of employment-related superannuation schemes had steadily increased due to their widespread use as a tax shelter by high earners. The trade unions had targeted superannuation as an unfair perk for higher income earners. Initially the idea was to extend some of these perks to the working classes. Legislation was introduced to ensure that when an employer offered an occupational superannuation scheme, all employees were able to join. Other problems associated with these schemes were also addressed through legislative reform. These include the long vesting periods and lack of portability of these schemes, as well as the almost unlimited tax-free windfalls available at retirement.

However, discussions about a national contributory social security system were given impetus by wage negotiations. One of the goals of the Labor government during the 1980s was to control inflation by dampening down wage demands, which were arbitrated centrally and tended to flow from one industry to another. In 1985, the Australian Council of Trade Unions agreed with the government to moderate income demands and to negotiate instead for improvements in the "social wage." A key element in these discussions was that productivity gains were to be converted into employer contributions payable into a superannuation scheme rather than being paid in the form of wage increases. As was noted earlier, superannuation refers to employer-based contributory tax-advantaged retirement incomes programs. Payments can be made either in the form of lump sums or as pensions. Australians have shown a distinct preference for the maintenance of lump sum payments at retirement, which the government is trying to control by introducing tax incentives to encourage the development of annuities.

This strategy was seen to be a positive solution for all concerned. Workers would obtain a fully vested portable superannuation savings fund that could be used to finance their retirement. Schemes were to be controlled by boards in which the membership was to be equally divided between representatives of employers and the unions. The funds were to be managed by the private sector with no government involvement in either setting benefits or guaranteeing the security of the schemes. This strategy gave the unions access to, and partial control of, potentially large sums of capital. The government realized one of its goals of increasing national savings and jointly with employer groups saw the advantage of increasing capital available for investment. The government was also keen to encourage self-provision for retirement, thereby reducing the high rate of reliance on general revenues to finance the Age Pension.

Encouraged by the government, legislation allowing for employer-based superannuation schemes was ratified by the Conciliation and Arbitration Commission in 1986. However, by 1990 the government and unions were dissatisfied with the slow rate at which employer-based superannuation schemes were being introduced. Accordingly, the decision was made to introduce legislation to require the creation of these schemes, which were to be fully vested and portable. The *Superannuation Guarantee Charge* (SGC) was introduced in 1992 with employer contributions set initially at 5 percent of salaries. The amount is scheduled to rise progressively to 9 percent by the year 2000.

Australia now has a three-tiered retirement incomes system. At the base is the Age Pension, which is a social assistance scheme available to everyone who meets the specified age and residence qualifications. The two additional tiers comprise compulsory superannuation (SGC) and contributory occupational superannuation. The majority of the work force now has superannuation through the Superannuation Guarantee Charge. However, it will take at least twenty years for these funds to mature to provide significant retirement incomes for most workers. Although superannuation is currently seen as a supplement to the basic Age Pension, there is an expectation that it will eventually replace the Age Pension (Dawkins, 1992).

The fact that Australia has chosen to initiate a new contributory retirement incomes system might suggest that social assistance will be superseded as a model of social security. The introduction of the Superannuation Guarantee Charge changes the societal compact that has been the characteristic of the Australian welfare state. It also addresses some of the criticisms of the social assistance model. In establishing a compulsory contributory retirement income system managed not by the government but by the private sector, it ensures that several of the government's economic restructuring goals are met. First, a significant component of government expenditure for welfare provision (namely, old-age income) is being moved from public to private sources (even though it is heavily subsidized through tax concessions). Second, a large, guaranteed and increasing sum of capital for private sector investment has been ensured. Third, a clear link is being established between "productive work" and social well-being.

One of the characteristics of the Australian Age Pension system has been the decoupling of the link between income in old age and employment and earnings during midlife. The Age Pension has been based upon a concept of economic need rather than income replacement. Its entitlement basis has been one of citizenship rather than economic contribution or an explicit reimbursement or repayment of one's labor force status during working life. The adoption of the principle of income replacement and linking income in old age to individual employment-based earnings during working life has major implications for low-paid workers and those with limited labor force involvement. The social convention by which women's employment and earnings capacity are subjugated to family responsibilities ensures that family income rather than women's own earnings are the determinant of living standards and economic well-being both before and after retirement age.

The Superannuation Guarantee Charge also diverges from internationally established social insurance principles by being privately managed and funded. Government mandated contributory social insurance schemes in other countries are managed by a government agency and have ensured some broadly redistributive principles in benefit structuring. This has ensured protection to those, namely women, with low or no entitlements due to limited labor force participation. The Age Pension will now presumably fill that gap. Using social assistance for this purpose may prove troubling as it has in the United States.

Public statements about the change in the retirement incomes system claim that the Age Pension will remain the core component of the retirement incomes system (Dawkins, 1992: 1–2). Nevertheless, there is concern about the future of the Age Pension. The discourse about the Age Pension is already beginning to change as a part of the strategy to sell the Superannuation Guarantee Charge to voters. This involves media attention on the future cost of an older population and questions about the ability of governments to finance the Age Pension at current levels in the future. Although fears about the abolition of the Age Pension seem to be unfounded, its role in the retirement incomes system will change. Whether it will continue to be seen as an entitlement as now, or whether it will become a residual payment, the last resort of those who have been unable to save for retirement though superannuation, remains to be seen.

ADVANTAGES AND DISADVANTAGES OF SOCIAL ASSISTANCE

Income security systems can be evaluated in terms of their adequacy, efficiency, and equity. These three criteria will be used to examine the use of the social assistance approach in the Australian Age Pension and to evaluate its effectiveness.

First, with regard to adequacy, the Age Pension has been criticized for the relatively low rate of benefit and its low rate of income replacement for the retired population (Schultz, Borowski, and Crown, 1991). This confuses the income security and income maintenance functions of social security. The Australian Age Pension has a goal of providing income security not earnings replacement. Community expectations about appropriate living standards are constantly increasing. Nevertheless, research on pension adequacy suggests that the Age Pension enables beneficiaries to live at an adequate although not necessarily excessively generous standard, while providing a safety net against poverty for the older population (Foster, 1988).

Adequacy cannot be evaluated only on the basis of benefit levels. Actual and anticipated expenditures must also be taken into account. These include needs for housing, health care, and social and community support. The majority of pensioners own their homes on which they pay reduced property taxes. As a result of substantial improvements in rent assistance, the majority of pensioners who are paying rent now spend less than 30 percent of their pension on housing payments (Prosser and Leeper, 1994).

Perhaps more importantly, Age Pensioners have the security of free or heavily subsidized health care, including acute treatment, rehabilitation, community-based and long-term residential care, and prescriptions and disability aides. Although forms of rationing other than price are used for health care services, the national health insurance system ensures that the risk of catastrophic and unpredictable health care expenses is not a major economic threat for which provision must be made through either private insurance or savings.

Second, efficiency criteria need to be considered. The efficiency of the Australian system relates to the extent to which benefits are targeted on those most in need. A particular goal of the system over the past decade has been to improve targeting (Baldwin, 1994). This relates to a changing view of the Age Pension over the past twenty years. During the 1970s, the pension was anticipated to expand to cover all Australians on the basis of entitlement. More recently, the strategy has been to develop it as a supplement to other retirement income and as the main support for a relatively small proportion of the retired population. The effectiveness of these strategies is clear in the reduction in coverage rates for the pension from 78 percent to 58 percent of the age eligible population.

Efficiency also relates to the administrative cost of the program. Programs that require income and asset tests need to be regularly reassessed and are generally more expensive to administer than those that are based upon a formula determined by prior contributions. Administrative resources must also be devoted to the detection of fraud and overpayments, in addition to ensuring that all those who may be eligible are aware of, and apply for the program. In this respect, the Australian pension system is not cheap, with administrative costs estimated at 3 percent of outlays (Australia, 1992b). Perhaps more significant, however, is the complexity of the system of payments, entitlements, income tests, asset tests, and deeming. Research indicates there are major confusions in older people's understanding of the income test, the interaction between the Age Pension and other forms of income, the assets tests, and the calculation of benefits (Barber, 1994). This confusion is costly in terms of loss of community support for the system, as well as discouraging eligible older people from applying.

One effect of the high coverage rate has been the lack of stigma associated with receipt of the Age Pension. Stigma can be inculcated by public statements and by negative administrative mechanisms. The Department of Social Security that administers the system prides itself on its humane administration. Its approach is to deliver social security entitlements with fairness, courtesy, and efficiency. This is encouraged through attempts at outreach through advertising, use of community languages, and flexible delivery systems for indigenous Australians. The Age Pension has been seen as a right rather than as a welfare benefit and one that all Australians are entitled to apply for as a result of their contributions as citizens.

A concern about social assistance is its disincentive effects on saving for retirement. The availability of the Age Pension as a safety net is often criticized as contributing to low rates of national savings, with a consequent need for Australia to borrow overseas to meet the need for development capital. The Treasurer in introducing the Superannuation Guarantee Charge asserted, "It will increase our national savings overall, thus reducing our reliance on the savings of foreigners to fund our development" (Dawkins, 1992). Whether it is the income security guaranteed through social assistance programs that reduces incentives for people to save, or whether it is lack of adequate income to enable people to save, or the typical easy-going Australian "they'll be right" approach is a moot point. Nevertheless, if one of the purposes of retirement incomes programs is to engender habits of saving, social assistance programs are clearly inefficient in this respect.

A third factor is the equity of the program. Equity requires that people in similar situations be treated similarly. Although the social assistance approach is usually regarded as being equitable on economic grounds, there are many areas in which issues of equity can be raised. These include equity between pensioners and self-funded retirees, equity between Age Pensioners and other social security beneficiaries, equity between aboriginal and non-aboriginal Australians, and equity between women and men.

The issue of equity between Age Pensioners and self-funded retirees has become a major issue as the number of older people retiring with employment-based superannuation grows. The additional noncash benefits that accrue to pensioners, and particularly the recent action to remove pensioners from the tax system, mean that age pensioners can in fact be much better off financially than nonpensioners who are receiving the same level of income. In addition, since the means test for pension eligibility assesses income and assets but not expenditures, self-funded retirees with major expenditures can in fact be financially disadvantaged relative to pensioners.

The high take-up rate of the pension among older people has led to Age Pensioners becoming a significant lobby group (Borowski, 1991). The strong voice of the aged makes politicians extremely sensitive to any proposals that might alienate older voters in general and Age Pensioners in particular. Since most working-age Australians are also currently likely to have a parent or grandparent who is a pensioner, it is a brave politician who criticizes the Age Pension directly. Consequently, attempts to reduce benefits, impose additional charges, or restrict eligibility have been difficult to enact. Often they have been considerably watered down. The aged are much more powerful politically than other social security beneficiaries.

With regard to equity between Age Pensioners and other social security beneficiaries, recent research indicates that the findings of the *1976 Poverty Report* that Age Pensioners were among the poorest groups in the population have now been addressed. This is in large part because of changes to the Age Pension during the past twenty years. The newer generations of the aged are also entering retirement with considerably higher assets and income sources that supplement the pension. Sole parents and families that have experienced unemployment during recent economic downturns have low or no assets or savings to fall back on and are much more likely to be living in poverty. Public attention is now being focused on poverty among these groups. Suggestions that the aged have done well out of the social welfare system and further demands from them are unjustified.

With regard to equity between specific groups of Australians, some commentators have suggested that certain groups of Australians benefit disproportionately from the Age Pension. Recognizing the poor health and high age mortality of aboriginal Australians, suggestions have been made that eligibility for the Age Pension among aboriginals should begin at forty or forty-five years of age in order to give them the opportunity to receive benefits on a similar basis to other Australians (McCallum, 1989).

The gender issue is somewhat different. Relative to men, women are more financially disadvantaged in old age. However, women pensioners outnumber men. Currently, 63.5 percent of women of pensionable age receive pensions compared to 49 percent of older men. A higher proportion of women receive the full pension with little or no supplementation from savings or investments. Alternatively, women benefit disproportionately from the age pension, due to their greater longevity and their lower age of eligibility. Both factors enable them to benefit for much longer periods than most men.

Equalizing the age of pension eligibility between women and men was addressed by the Social Security Review. A key recommendation was that male and female pensionable ages should be equalized once greater labor market and pay equality had been attained. Despite continuing evidence of significant labor market and pay disparities between women and men, the government in 1993 formulated proposals for the gradual phasing in of a standard age of pension eligibility of sixty-five for both men and women. This decision can be seen as part of an overall movement to eliminate gender-based differentiation in the administration of the social security system despite continuing labor market and pay differentials between women and men.

CONCLUSION: RELEVANCE TO OTHER COUNTRIES

The many changes to social security protection for the elderly introduced during the past decade raise questions about the future of social assistance in societies faced with aging populations and governments that are attempting to limit expenditures. Members of the Australian government and key commentators have argued that the issue is not whether the Age Pension will continue but how it can best be integrated with the national superannuation system.

Whether the Australian social assistance model is appropriate for other countries depends very much on their demographic features, stage of economic and social development, current structure of social and economic support for the aged, and expectations about future labor market and economic changes. Social security systems, like many other institutions, are based on the social values of the society and are molded by economic and political imperatives. Societies should develop social security systems that are consonant with their social and economic systems and with their stage of development.

Social assistance provisions for retirement are particularly appropriate in societies that are relatively young demographically, in which disposable incomes are low, and where self-employment and extensive migration flows are common. The use of social assistance to provide retirement pensions in India and South Africa seem, therefore, to be appropriate. In advanced industrial and postindustrial societies with high levels of disposable income, and with aging populations, the need to adopt contributory insurance systems has been accepted. Such systems, particularly when managed by the private sector, reduce the growth in government expenditures and provide a source of development capital.

However, social assistance schemes will always be needed to compensate for the basic inequities inherent in social insurance models. These include supplementing retirement incomes for those whose labor force participation has been limited and whose earnings have been low. Changing patterns of work in postindustrial societies suggest that part-time and casual work, early retirement, and low-wage employment are increasing. In view of these realities, the need for equitable, adequate, and nonstigmatizing social assistance schemes is likely to increase. Social assistance should be viewed as a viable approach, particularly when applied effectively to address the needs of the most disadvantaged.

REFERENCES

Australia, Bureau of Immigration Research (1992a) *Australia's population trends and prospects 1992*. Canberra: Australian Government Publishing Service.

Australia, Department of Social Security (1992b) Developments in the social security system since 1983. *International Social Security Review* 45(3): 83–89.

Baldwin, P. (1994) Progress and prospects in social security policy. In *Social security policy: Issues and options*, eds. J. Disney and L. Briggs. Canberra: Australian Government Publishing Service, 1–5.

Barber, J. (1994) Pension means test: Successes, problems and prospects. In *Social security policy: Issues and options*, eds. J. Disney and L. Briggs. Canberra: Australian Government Publishing Service, 155–65.

Borowski, A. (1991) The economics and politics of retirement incomes policy. *Australia International Social Security Review* 44(1): 27–40.

Brown, R. (1994) Integration of public and private provision for retirement. In *Social security policy: Issues and options*, eds. J. Disney and L. Briggs. Canberra: Australian Government Publishing Service, 143–54.

Cass, B. (1990) Reforming family income support, reforming labour markets: Pursuing social justice in Australia in the 1980s. In *Social policy review, 1989–1990*, eds. N. Manning and C. Ungerson. London: Longman, 187–213.

Cass, B. (1994) Social security policy into the twenty-first century. In *Social security policy: Issues and options*, eds. J. Disney and L. Briggs. Canberra: Australian Government Publishing Service, 15–28.

Dawkins, J. (1992) *Security in retirement: Planning for tomorrow today*. Canberra: Australian Government Publishing Service.

Foster, C. (1988) *Towards a national retirement incomes policy*. Social Security Review Issues Paper No. 6. Department of Social Security, Canberra.

James, E. (1994) *Averting the old age crisis*. Washington, D.C.: World Bank.

McCallum, J. (1989) *The Public versus the policies: The Ethical basis of Australian retirement income policy*. Working Paper No. 7. Canberra: National Centre for Epidemiology and Population Health, Australian National University.

Prosser B., and G. Leeper (1994) Housing affordability and rent assistance. *Social Security Journal* (June); 40–62.

Pusey, M. (1991) *Economic rationalism in Canberra: A nation building state changes its mind*. Melbourne: Cambridge University Press.

Rosenman, L. (1994) Changing labour force involvement, early retirement and superannuation. In *Social security policy: Issues and options*, eds. J. Disney and L. Briggs. Canberra: Australian Government Publishing Service, 167–75.

Schultz, J., Borowski, A., and W. Crown (1991) *Economics of population aging: The "graying" of Australia, Japan and the United States*. Westport, Conn.: Auburn House.

Winocur, S., Rosenman, L., and J. Warburton (1994) *Retirement decisions of women from a non-English speaking background*. Canberra: Bureau of Immigration and Population Research. Australian Government Publishing Service.

3

Provident Funds and Social Protection: The Case of Singapore

Michael Sherraden

Singapore has been much in the news in recent years for its preoccupation with civil order, repression of speech, and hard positions on punishment. These matters merit our attention, but they are not the only interesting things about Singapore. Singapore is unusual in many, many ways. Since the beginning of self rule in 1959, it has been remarkably open to social and economic experimentation. In some respects Singapore is almost a laboratory for unusual domestic policies, some successful and others not so successful, but almost all of them interesting. As we look at this tiny innovative nation, there is a great deal to consider other than authoritarianism and public order. From the viewpoint of the United States, some areas where we should pay particular attention are the high rate of savings and economic growth, the organization of social policy, and how the two are interrelated.

The Central Provident Fund (CPF) of Singapore is a state-sponsored system of compulsory savings accounts. It is the world's most extensive example of social policy based on assets. Singapore stands in marked contrast to Western welfare states, where social policy is based primarily on social insurance and income transfer. The perspectives underlying these two types of policies could hardly be more different: In the West, we think of social policy as income for consumption that we enjoy because the economy is productive enough to be taxed for social spending. In Singapore, social policy is not separated from economic policy. The CPF is used to accumulate capital that in turn has multiple positive effects, both social and economic, for households and the nation as a whole. The idea that social policy can be a mechanism for capital accumulation and investment is taken for granted in Singapore, but it seems somewhat contradictory in the West.

CPF accounts are used for a wide range of social and economic purposes, including retirement security, home ownership, medical care, life and health insurances, education, and several types of investments. Altogether, the CPF is a broad domestic policy system that plays a central role in Singapore's society and economy. Among other things, the CPF is widely credited with a dramatic increase in the rate of home ownership (now exceeding 92 percent, the highest in the world). In addition, the substantial pool of capital accumulated in CPF accounts has been a key factor in Singapore's economic growth and stability.

Unfortunately, to date very little is known about the CPF in Western Europe and North America. Only a handful of scholars are knowledgeable about provident funds, and almost no research-based articles on CPF or provident funds are published in Western journals. In discussions of social policy in the United States, the Singapore example is rarely mentioned, and no systematic research has been available. Nor has any previously published study been based on systematic data collected independently by outside researchers.

A number of scholars have written generally about the CPF as a social security or social welfare system (Asher, 1991; Chow, 1981, Jones, 1990; Kalirajan and Wiboonchutikula, 1986; Liew, 1992, Lim L., 1989; Tyabji, 1986; Queisser, 1991). Others have addressed accountancy issues such as contribution rates, partitions into accounts, or interest rates (CPF Board, 1955–1992, Central Provident Fund Study Group, 1986; Iau, 1979, Deutsch and Zowall, 1988); coverage and adequacy issues (Asher, 1991; Liew, 1992), or microeconomic effects on households and businesses (Wee and Han, 1983; Krause et al., 1987); macroeconomic impacts of the CPF (Asher, 1983; Central Provident Fund Study Group, 1986; Goh K.S., 1977; Lim C.Y., 1988; Pugh, 1984; Shome and Saito, 1985); and particular policy areas, such as aging (Cheung, 1992; Republic of Singapore, 1984, 1989), housing (Chua, 1988; Goh K.S., 1956; Goh L.E., 1988; Pugh, 1987; Tan and Phang, 1991; Tracy 1992; Wong and Yeh, 1985; Yeh, 1975), and health care (Phua, 1991; Republic of Singapore, 1992; Toh and Low, 1991). However, in these studies, there has been no careful assessment of how the CPF has been used by Singaporeans, or on its impact as Singapore's primary social policy instrument. In this chapter I take up topics that have been somewhat overlooked in the past: changes and development of CPF schemes over time and how the CPF has been used by Singaporeans and its impact as Singapore's primary social policy instrument.

STUDY METHODS

Several study methods were employed during residence in Singapore during 1992 and 1993, with follow-up data collected thereafter: (1) review of all available documentary evidence; (2) interviews with key policy makers, CPF program officials, and CPF scholars; (3) analysis of macro program data provided by the CPF Board; (4) focus group discussions with different segments of the Singapore population by race/ethnicity and income levels (11 groups); and (5) a face-to-face in-home survey with a random sample of CPF members (N = 356, response rate 79.1 percent). These multiple research approaches have been important in order to "see" the CPF from different perspectives and obtain a balanced overall understanding. This chapter is a brief summary of some of the research findings regarding policy development and impacts of the CPF[1].

ORIGIN AND DEVELOPMENT OF PROVIDENT FUNDS

Before turning to the CPF, it is useful to say a few words about provident funds in general. Provident funds are a form of social security run by the state on principles of defined contribution, that is, each individual has an account wherein deposits and earnings accumulate on an individual basis. Typically deposits come from a combination of employer and employee contributions, with a state subsidy in the form of tax benefits. Provident funds, like social insurance, are typically (though not necessarily) mandatory. Provident funds have been used primarily for retirement security, but some countries have used provident funds for other social policy purposes as well, especially housing (Tracy, 1992).

Provident funds were initiated by British colonial authorities in Africa, South Asia, and Southeast Asia (Dixon 1989a, 1989b; Friedman, 1989; International Social Security Association, 1965; International Social Security Association, 1975–present). The British viewed provident funds as inferior social policy schemes, but they instituted provident funds in the colonies because they did not want to take on the long-term financial obligations of social insurance.

Most provident funds were started during the 1950s, but some of these, particularly in Africa, were unsuccessful and no longer exist. Others have emerged in the 1960s, 1970s, and 1980s, notably in a number of the Pacific Islands. In 1989, countries with national provident funds for "old age, invalidity, and death" included Fiji, Gambia, India (with many other arrangements as well), Indonesia, Kenya, Kiribati (Gilbert Islands), Malaysia (along with social insurance for invalidity), Nepal, Nigeria, Papua New Guinea, Singapore, Solomon Islands, Sri Lanka, Swaziland, Tanzania, Thailand (for public employees only), Uganda, Vanautu, Western Samoa, Yemen Arab Republic (which began in 1988), and Zambia, for a total of twenty-one countries (U.S. Department of Health and Human Services, 1990).

In the first regional meeting of the International Social Security Administration (ISSA) for Asia and Oceania, held in Tokyo in 1962, the view of provident funds was that they were temporary, transitional social security models on the way to becoming insurance-based social security systems. One of the papers, prepared by the General Secretariat of the ISSA, was entitled "Working Paper on Technical Problems Involved in the Transition from Provident Funds to Pensions Insurance." This paper cited a "minimum standard" that had been set by a Social Security Convention in 1952 that "requires that the transition should, sooner or later, be effected, because central provident funds are primitive and inadequate as means to social security in comparison with pension systems."

The dominant view among welfare policy analysts has been that social insurance schemes are superior to provident funds. In a major survey of programs throughout the world (U.S. Department of Health and Human Services, 1990), no particular attention is given to provident funds, and social security is literally defined as programs that "insure" against various conditions (old age, disability, death, unemployment). Public provident funds are barely mentioned and said to "exist in developing countries." Provident funds also have been generally downplayed by the Organization for Economic Cooperation and Development (OECD), the International Social Security Association (ISSA), and the International Labour Office (ILO). These international organizations are concerned, with good reason, about the coverage and adequacy of provident funds and are generally opposed to the principle of strictly relating contributions to benefits.

Looking at reports of the ISSA Committee on Provident Funds, the first meeting in 1975 in Lusaka was dominated by discussion of the transformation of provident funds into pension schemes, and this topic appeared again in 1979, 1982, 1986, and 1991. But with the passage of time, this theme has diminished in prominence. Administrative and management issues—morganization, decentralization, personnel, collections and enforcement, record keeping, data processing—mare the most numerous topics in recent years. As time has passed provident funds have gained a permanent status. For example, extension of scope and coverage were themes in 1982 and 1988, and in 1991 there was a session on the role and potential of provident funds in national economic and financial systems, indicating that the programs were no longer seen to be merely temporary (ISSA, Committee on Provident Funds, various years).

To be sure, provident funds are not without problems. Indeed, many of the British colonial funds have been failures. Dangers include the prevalent depreciation of currency in many developing countries, which has severe effects on the adequacy of the eventual support; poor management and/or corruption in overseeing the funds and their administration; and "social inefficiency" due to wastage of lump-sum payments at retirement. "It is held against provident funds that a lump-sum payment could be squandered away, compared with periodic payments, and that when the membership is of a short duration, the benefit is inadequate in such contingencies as death and incapacity" (Yee, 1991). The lack of sophistication in handling large sums of money and imprudent spending habits have sometimes been mentioned in quite paternalistic terms (ISSA, 1962).

Despite these concerns, and despite the conventional wisdom that provident funds would eventually fade away, they are instead beginning to stage somewhat of a resurgence. In particular, successes in Singapore and Malaysia have influenced provident fund development in the Pacific Islands, and it is possible that Singapore's CPF will have a major influence on Chinese policy development and policy development elsewhere in East and Southeast Asia.

Singapore is the most exceptional and influential case, with the largest and most comprehensive provident fund. Over the years, the CPF has been shaped into something far more extensive and permanent than the minimal and temporary old-age scheme that British colonial authorities had in mind. In retrospect, the British instituted provident funds, which they viewed as inferior, while for themselves they chose social pensions. The colonial structure, as is true of any imperialist structure, pulled wealth from the colonies to help finance the British welfare state. But with the unraveling of the colonial empire, the social policies that it supported have begun to unravel as well. Ironically, in Singapore the supposedly inferior system that the British promoted has become a capital accumulation mechanism that has helped finance remarkable economic growth and become a very effective social policy instrument. Today the British welfare state faces growing pressures, while the CPF is robust and prospering. This is an irony that is not lost on Singaporeans. But whether or not provident funds are a desirable policy option for other countries remains an open question.

CPF STRUCTURE, HISTORY, POLICY CHANGE, AND SOCIAL IMPACT

The CPF has gradually been changed from a simple retirement scheme into a comprehensive domestic policy system based on individual savings. As such, it is highly unique. No other country has such an extensive domestic policy based on individual savings. In this section we examine CPF policies and schemes to see how the CPF has developed over time and how it is used by Singaporeans. Of particular interest is the social impact of the CPF, not only in retirement support, but also in housing, health care, insurances, investments, and other areas in which the CPF has come to play a central role.

Policy Structure

Deposits into CPF accounts are made by employers and employees, and deposits currently total 40 percent of wages, up to a monthly salary ceiling of $6,000 (all money figures in this report are in Singapore dollars; at this writing one U.S. dollar is equal to about 1.4 Singapore dollars). CPF contributions are compulsory for most employees and their employers.

CPF savings are completely tax exempt, both at the time of deposit and withdrawal. Within restrictions, CPF accounts are used for home ownership, education, medical care, retirement security, home insurance, life insurance, and other social and economic purposes. All CPF schemes are administered directly by the Central Provident Fund Board and are specified by the 1953 Central Provident Fund Act and its amendments.

The individual is the basic unit, although there are certain mechanisms for family members to assist one another. Provident funds are often said to be based on individual or family responsibility, in contrast to Western welfare states, which rely primarily on public support through some combination of social insurance and income transfer.

CPF savings are managed by the CPF Board, which has a very conservative investment strategy of purchasing mostly Singapore government securities: "We provide fair market returns at minimal risk. . . . The guiding principle is prudence" (CPF Board, *Annual Report 1991*; 1). In turn, the Singapore government invests the funds. Details of the government's investments are hidden, but it is clear that CPF funds have contributed substantially to the building up of Singapore's foreign reserves, which are the highest per capita in the world.

The key characteristics of CPF are (1) individual accounts; (2) defined contributions (rather than defined benefits); (3) funded accounts (rather than "pay as you go"); (4) partitioned accounts with funds segregated for different purposes; and (5) complete portability of benefits from one employer to another. In many respects, CPF is simple in design and function. Members have fully owned accounts, backed by government reserves, and the accumulated money can be used, within stated guidelines, for a variety of social and economic purposes. Members make individualized decisions about the use of their funds, and when compared to most social policy systems elsewhere, bureaucratic layers of policy implementation are largely avoided. As detailed below, the basic structure of the CPF has proven to be flexible in accommodating a wide range of new policy directions through the creation of different schemes for the use of CPF funds.

The CPF is sometimes described in the West as "forced savings," although there is nothing more forced about it than Social Security in the United States, or any other mandated tax for social purposes. What is different about the CPF is the large size of the contributions and individual, funded accounts rather than unfunded social insurance.

Goals and Objectives

The original and still central goal of the Central Provident Fund is to assist wage earners, through individual savings, to achieve a measure of financial security and to provide a safety net for workers and family members in the event of permanent disability or death. Initially the primary objective was old-age protection. Over the years, however, the CPF has evolved to include more comprehensive objectives. In particular, the CPF has taken on major commitments in housing and health care, and more recently in protection in the event of personal catastrophe. At present, there are four primary objectives: (1) old-age financial security, aiming for retirement security equivalent to 20 to 40 percent of last-drawn pay; (2) home ownership for as many families as possible, aiming for a fully paid home at retirement; (3) a medical account for health care at retirement; and (4) protection in the event of catastrophe, aiming for a combination of lump-sum payment, back-up income support, and insurances (CPF Board, *Annual Report 1990*, 3). How these specific objectives—particularly the 20 to 40 percent of last-drawn pay—are estimated by the CPF Board is unclear.

As described below, the CPF has taken on other objectives as well, notably the economic objective of higher earnings through investment schemes. The manner in which the CPF attempts to achieve these multiple objectives can be understood through the CPF schemes, which are described below.

Program Scope

At the end of 1993, the CPF had a total of $52.3 billion in member accounts. A total of $10.2 billion in contributions were credited during the year, offset by $10.9 billion in withdrawals (at least $5.6 billion of the withdrawals in 1993 were for investment schemes).

The contribution rates in 1993 were 18.5 percent of wages from the employer, and 21.5 percent from the employee. The stated long-term goal is to reach a balance of 20 percent each, and keep the total at 40 percent. In the past, the government has changed contribution rates for macroeconomic reasons (most notably a 15 percent reduction in the employer's rate during a recession in 1985), but the official position today is that the government will avoid making changes in contribution rates in the future. Unofficially, top political leaders suggest otherwise—that the CPF will, if it becomes necessary, be used to make macroeconomic adjustments. At the end of 1993 there were 2.4 million CPF members, slightly more male than female, and 1.1 million of these were active members, namely, they actively contributed to their accounts during the past year.

Not all employees and very few of the self-employed fully participate in the CPF. Asher (1992) reports that as of 1991 only about 69 percent of the employed labor force was participating in the CPF (down from a peak of almost 84 percent in 1981). Non-participants include migrant contract labor, who are not covered by the CPF, and some other day laborers and their employers who, despite enforcement measures, find a way to avoid participation. On the other hand, since July 1992 the self-employed have been required to contribute to Medisave (see below), and the unofficial long-term plan is to "bring them in" as fully participating CPF members.

CPF funds are partitioned into four types of accounts (Ordinary, Special, Medisave, and Retirement), and they are accessed by members through more than a dozen schemes designed for a wide range of social and economic purposes.

Policy Change: Development of CPF Schemes

The CPF began in 1955 under the British colonial government as a simple "provident fund" to provide a lump-sum payment to workers at age fifty-five or in the case of death or permanent disability. In the early years, the amount was smaller (a total of 10 percent of wages), and the CPF was known among Singaporeans as "coffin money." When Singapore initiated self-rule in 1959, the CPF was relatively insignificant and remained so for some time. Political turmoil and geopolitical vulnerability dominated Singapore's transition into a fully independent nation in 1965. It was not until well after this period, beginning in 1968, that Prime Minister Lee Kuan Yew and his chief economic adviser Goh Keng Swee began to institute policies that expanded and fundamentally changed the nature of the CPF. Since that time, the CPF has evolved into a multifaceted policy instrument with many different schemes. A summary of CPF schemes is presented in Table 3.1. There is not space here to describe CPF schemes in detail—each is an interesting story in its own right—but summary observations may be useful.

Provident Fund (1955). As described above, the major objective is to build up enough savings to sustain the member during retirement. A secondary objective is to provide at least partial support for the family in the case of death or permanent incapacity.

Public Housing (1968). In 1968 came the first major departure from the original provident fund idea, permitting withdrawals before age fifty five for the purchase of public housing. As a result of the Public Housing Scheme, most Singaporeans assume that they will be able to own a property. Prices are heavily subsidized at the bottom. Today housing equity is the largest component of net worth for the average Singaporean and home ownership has been, without doubt, the most pronounced impact of the CPF.

Singapore Bus Service (SBS) Shares (1978). Government officials decided

Table 3.1
Central Provident Fund Schemes

CPF Scheme	Date Introduced	Social Objective	Policy Mechanism
Provident Fund	1955	Retirement and family security	Individual savings
Public Housing	1968	Housing and investment	Home ownership
Singapore Bus Service Shares	1978	Investment and transportation	Share ownership
Residential Properties	1981	Housing and investment	Home ownership
Home Protection	1981	Family Security	Insurance
Company Welfarism Through Employers' Contributions (CoWEC)	1983	Companies decide on use of funds	Pooled fund at company level
Medisave	1984	Health care	Individual savings and intra-family transfer
Non-Residential Properties	1986	Investment	Property ownership
Investment	1986	Investment	Securities ownership
Minimum Sum	1987	Retirement security	Forced annuity and intra-family transfer
Dependent Protection	1989	Family security	Insurance
Education	1989	Tertiary education	Loan and intra-family support
Medishield	1990	Health care	Insurance
Shares Top-Up	1993	Investment	Matching grant for securities ownership

to take over several small private bus companies and combine them into a more efficient publicly traded company. CPF members were allowed to use their accounts to purchase shares, creating the first CPF investment scheme.

Residential Properties (1981). This scheme enables Singaporeans to use their CPF savings to buy private residential properties to live in, or to own for investment income and capital appreciation.

Home Protection (1981). The Home Protection Scheme was the first CPF insurance scheme. This compulsory mortgage-reducing plan protects members and their families from loss of their homes when members die or are permanently disabled. In effect, the Home Protection Scheme builds on and expands the original provident fund goal of family protection in the case of death or disability.

Company Welfarism through Employers' Contributions (CoWEC) (1983). Co-WEC allows an employer to retain 7 percent of wages from the CPF contribution that would ordinarily be submitted to the CPF Board. The retained contributions go to a parallel, company-based scheme. From a policy analysis standpoint, it is important to note that CoWEC represents a fundamentally different social policy approach, a step toward "occupational welfare" in hopes of increasing productivity. CoWEC is notable in that it is the only CPF scheme introduced to date that is much less successful than was originally hoped—indeed, it is pretty much a failure.

Medisave (1984). Medisave is an application of the provident fund concept to health care, designed to enable Singaporeans to save toward hospitalization needs. Medisave is the world's only national program using individual savings accounts for health coverage, and Singapore's total expenditure on health care runs about 3.1 percent of GDP, which is exceptionally low for a developed country.

Investment (1986). The Investment Scheme was designed in part to free up CPF funds for investment in the Singapore stock market, which was depressed at the time. The Investment Scheme was also a response to pressure from a growing managerial and professional class to loosen control over their substantial CPF savings. In 1993 rules were announced for a revised Basic Investment Scheme and a new Enhanced Investment Scheme that freed more capital for share investment.

Non-Residential Properties (1986). Non-Residential Properties was the third investment scheme offered by the CPF. It was designed for use in purchasing commercial properties as either an active or a passive investment.

Minimum Sum (1987). The Minimum Sum Scheme is a forced annuity that seeks to ensure that CPF members have at least a small but steady monthly income after the age of sixty. In 1994 it was announced that the minimum sum would be gradually increased for added protection.

Education (1989). The Education Scheme allows members to use up to 40 percent of their investable savings to pay for their own or their children's tertiary education. It is a loan scheme in that the amount borrowed from the CPF account must be paid back, with interest, following graduation.

Dependent Protection (1989). The Dependent Protection Scheme was introduced as an optional life insurance scheme. About 80 percent of eligible CPF members are covered, and the remaining 20 percent have opted out because they have their own life insurance, are unable to pay the premium, or hold personal or religious objections to insurance.

Medishield (1990). Medishield is designed as low-cost catastrophic illness insurance, giving extended illness coverage to members and their dependents. Medishield Plus was introduced in 1994, effectively splitting Medishield into a two-tier program. The regular Medishield has lower premiums and serves lower-class hospital wards, while Medishield Plus has higher premiums and serves the higher-class wards (Singapore has explicitly tiered hospitalization, with heavily subsidized basic care at the bottom).

Shares Top-Up, or Special Discounted Shares (1993). "In line with the announced intention to turn Singapore into a share-owning society," a CPF top-up scheme was implemented, putting $200 into the CPF account of each Singaporean CPF member aged twenty-one and above who had recently contributed at least $500 to their accounts, or to previous nonmembers if they deposited $500, all for the purpose of purchasing the newly privatized Telecom shares at a discount.

Key Policy Decisions

It is useful to summarize key CPF policy decisions over time. In retrospect, eight key policy decision points can be identified. The first key decision was made in 1959 (the date of self-rule and election of the People's Action Party government), when the leaders decided not to switch the CPF to a social insurance system, despite considerable pressure from the International Labour Office and other international entities to do so. This discussion was entertained in Singapore, but Dr. Goh Keng Swee and Senior Minister Lee Kuan say that they "never considered it." The primary reason was that they had too much else to think about at the time, but the decision proved to be a most important one: it left the CPF structure in place for later changes.

The second key decision, made in 1968, was to expand the CPF into housing. According to Lee Kuan Yew (personal interview), this decision was driven by considerations of national security. Singapore had been expelled from the Malaya Federation in 1965 and was a tiny and vulnerable nation, with potential for conflicts with both Malaysia and Indonesia. National security was paramount but the population did not strongly identify with being Singaporean. Prime Minister Lee decided that if people owned their own homes they would be more likely to fight for the country. Singapore has not had to fight a major war, but the home ownership policy has undoubtedly contributed to nation building. The strategic and domestic interests have been entirely complementary.

The third key decision, also made in 1968, was to begin expanding the contribution rate from a total of 10 percent of wages to an eventual high of 50 percent in 1985 (today the rate is 40 percent). This enabled CPF accounts to grow so that homes could be purchased, and eventually other

CPF schemes could be added as well. Perhaps more importantly, the draw-ing off of a gradually increasing percentage of earnings (at the same time being careful never to reduce real take-home pay) allowed the Singapore economy—and incomes—to grow rapidly without suffering inflationary pressures from rising wages available for consumption. This decision was guided by a combination of macroeconomic astuteness and Confucian austerity (in the West we would call it Puritanism). The old leadership (particularly Lee and Goh) had struggled dollar by dollar to build their country; the idea of mass consumption was (and remains) almost appall-ing to them. Better to save the money.

The fourth key decision was the 1978 move into SBS Shares as the first investment scheme. Although the SBS Shares program has not had a large impact in recent years, it set the stage for other investment schemes. By the 1990s, Prime Minster Goh Chok Tong had identified widespread share ownership as the next major thrust in asset building among Singaporeans. This is likely to be a major theme during the remainder of the twentieth century and beyond. The fifth key decision was the 1981 move into the Home Protection Scheme, signaling the expansion of the CPF into insur-ance. This has led to other life and medical insurance schemes. These are modeled on private insurance principles, (i.e., without cross-subsidization). But the insurance schemes provide significant "back-up" protections in a policy structure that does not have social insurances.

The sixth key decision was the 1984 move into health care with the Medisave Scheme. Medisave has been successful in helping to control health-care spending. As the world looks for solutions to rising health-care costs, it is likely that Medisave will receive far more attention in the future. The seventh key decision was the 1987 move to the Minimum Sum Scheme. This forced annuity provides another measure of protection against financial disaster. It is part of a trend in the CPF away from rank individualism and toward structured protections. Over the next several years, the Minimum Sum will be expanded to increase these protections.

The eighth key decision occurred in 1993 with Edusave (not officially part of the CPF) and the Shares Top-Up Scheme. These represent the first non-work-related funding of accounts, that is, the government is help-ing build accounts in ways that are not tied directly to employment. If asset-based policy is to be successful in covering an entire population (whether in Singapore or elsewhere), creative ways will have to be found to fund accounts for the poorest and non-working members of society. Singapore has taken small steps in this direction.

SOCIAL IMPACT

In a fundamental sense, CPF policy can best be understood by what it does for members, and what it does for members can be represented by

Table 3.2
Total CPF Withdrawals (Net of Refunds)
1993, millions of dollars

Category and Scheme	Amount	Percent of Total
Lump Sum Provident Fund*		
Age 55	$ 927.9	8.5
Leaving Singapore	178.0	1.6
Death and Disability	81.1	0.7
Income Protection		
Minimum Sum	122.3	1.1
Housing		
Public Housing	1,821.8	16.6
Residential Properties	1,687.6	15.4
Health Care		
Medisave	250.2	2.3
Insurances		
Home Protection	62.8	0.6
Dependent Protection	57.3	0.5
Medishield	41.9	0.4
Education		
Education	27.5	0.3
Investments		
Non-Residential Prop.	47.0	0.4
SBS Shares	(2.8)	(0.0)
Investment	4,129.3	37.7
Special Discounted Shares	1,512.0	13.8
TOTAL	10,943.9	100.0

Source: *Annual Report 1993*, CPF Board.

*Lump Sum category refers to provisions in Section 15 of CPF Act.

how the CPF funds are used. The use of funds can be tracked by annual withdrawals for different purposes, and the CPF's social impact is reflected in the pattern of withdrawals. This is not policy as someone may have intended but policy as it *actually operates* in Singaporean households and communities. In this section, we look at withdrawals by function.

Withdrawals in a Given Year

We turn first to withdrawals in a given year. Table 3.2 summarizes net withdrawals in 1993, showing the amount and percentage for each major scheme. The total withdrawn during 1993 was $10,943.9 million. Of this total, it is most striking that share investment (Investment Scheme and Special Discounted Shares Scheme) accounted for 51.5 percent of the total. This was a dramatic change from 1992, spurred by changes in 1993 in the rules and incentives for share investments in the CPF. As of 1993, the CPF had become a major engine for share ownership by the Singaporean population.

The two housing schemes (Public Housing and Residential Property) accounted for 32.0 percent of all withdrawals. The original lump-sum provident fund schemes (Age 55, Leaving Singapore, Death and Disability) together accounted for only 10.8 percent of withdrawals. In other words, as measured by dollars withdrawn during 1993, the impact of housing schemes was about three times as great as that of the lump-sum provident fund. Making up a smaller proportion of total withdrawals is the health care scheme (Medisave) at 2.3 percent. The remainder of the schemes make up still smaller percentages: insurances (Home Protection, Dependents' Protection, and Medishield) accounted for 1.5 percent; income protection (Minimum Sum) accounted for 1.1 percent; and the Education Scheme accounted for only 0.3 percent.

Overall, we can say that what today's CPF does foremost for Singaporeans is share investment and housing. Old-age security, at this time, plays a distant tertiary role (although share investment and housing can also be considered important forms of old-age security). Health care comes next, while insurances, income protection, and education are relatively minor schemes in terms of dollars spent.

Withdrawals by Social Objective

At this point, it may be helpful to summarize CPF withdrawals over time, but to do so from a slightly different perspective. In keeping with a central theme of this chapter, we now look at CPF withdrawals not exactly by types of schemes, but rather by the general social objective that they seek to promote. Taking this viewpoint requires us to rearrange schemes into slightly different categories: retirement, family protection, health care, housing, investments, and education. Table 3.3 presents annual withdrawals in these categories between 1960 and 1993, and provides the single most concise summary of what the CPF has been doing for Singaporeans since it began forty years ago under the British colonial government. First we can look at total withdrawals, which grew from a mere $3.9 million in 1960 to a three thousand-fold increase of $10,943.9 million in 1990 (the total dollar figure is slightly different depending on which CPF Board figures one uses). In 1990 (before investments played a major role in CPF withdrawals) total CPF withdrawals were about 6.9 percent of GDP. Looking at this figure in terms of social impact, it was more money than the Singapore government spent for all recurrent expenditures in social

Table 3.3
Summary of Annual CPF Withdrawals* by Social Objective**
1960–1990, millions of dollars (percentages)

Year	Retirement	Family Security	Housing	Investment	Health Care	Education	Total
1960	3.4 (87.2)	0.5 (12.8)	--	--	--	--	3.9 (100.0)
1965	8.0 (86.0)	1.3 (14.0)	--	--	--	--	9.3 (100.0)
1970	19.6 (43.5)	2.6 (5.7)	22.9 (50.8)	--	--	--	45.1 (100.0)
1975	72.7 (33.5)	9.8 (4.5)	134.8 (62.0)	--	--	--	217.3 (100.0)
1980	237.2 (30.4)	19.0 (2.4)	520.9 (66.9)	1.9 (0.2)	--	--	779.0 (100.0)
1985	652.6 (19.4)	94.0 (2.8)	2,556.4 (76.4)	2.6 (0.1)	43.9 (1.3)	--	3,359.2 (100.0)
1990	1,025.5 (25.9)	83.1 (2.1)	2,259.1 (57.2)	332.3 (8.4)	240.1 (6.1)	11.9 (0.3)	3,952.0 (100.0)
1993	1,228.2 (11.2)	201.2 (1.8)	3,509.4 (32.1)	5,685.5 (52.0)	292.1 (2.7)	27.5 (0.2)	10,943.9 (100.0)

Source: *Annual Reports*, CPF Board.

* Includes all withdrawals of money that actually reaches the CPF Board. Does not include money withheld at the company level for the CoWEC scheme, nor any non-CPF collections.

** Social objectives listed are comprised of the following CPF schemes:
Retirement = Age 55, Minimum Sum, Leaving Singapore
Family Security = Death, Disability, Home Protection, Dependent Protection
Housing = Public Housing, Residential Properties
Investment = SBS Shares, Non-Residential Properties, Investment, Special Discounted Shares
Health = Medisave, Medishield
Education = Education

and community policy (including education, health, community development, information and the arts, environment, and public housing) during the same year. Therefore, as measured by dollars applied, the CPF has far and away the greatest impact of any domestic social policy. It casts a very large shadow over everything else.

Turning next to what social objectives were being addressed by CPF withdrawals, in 1960 and 1965, in keeping with the original provident fund concept, more than 85 percent of the withdrawals were for retirement, and the remainder were for family security. By 1970 a dramatic change was occurring. The Public Housing Scheme had been introduced in 1968 and within two years it already represented 50.8 percent of all CPF withdrawals, and this figure rose to a remarkable 76.4 percent by 1985. Thus, when the CPF outgrew its narrow provident fund beginnings, the simple retirement fund—often derided as "coffin money"—took wing and facilitated a huge housing program, transforming Singapore in the process, both physically and socially. We do not have space in this report to describe housing policy in detail (see Chua, 1988; Goh K.S., 1956; Goh L.E., 1988; Pugh, 1987; Tan and Phang, 1991; Tracy, 1992; Wong and Yeh, 1985; Yeh, 1975). However, the amount of expenditure compared to GDP, and the substantial transformation of rural kampong areas and urban slums into high-rise apartments, more than 90 percent owned by Singaporeans, must qualify Singapore's housing policy, on a per capita basis, as one of the most comprehensive ever undertaken.

From 1970 through 1985 retirement played an ever-declining role relative to housing, although absolute withdrawal amounts continued to rise. With a changing age structure, however, this pattern was reversed by 1990, when retirement accounted for 25.9 percent of all withdrawals. As the population continues to age, withdrawals for retirement are likely to rise during coming decades.

Family security has continued to decline in emphasis, falling to 1.8 percent of withdrawals by 1993. With the increasing general good health of the population, and decreasing physical danger in employment for Singaporean citizens, family security withdrawals will probably continue to remain at modest levels in the years ahead.

Investment started with the SBS Shares Scheme in 1978, but accounted for only 0.2 percent of all withdrawals by 1980, and an even smaller 0.1 percent by 1985. However, after the Non-Residential Properties and Investment Scheme were introduced in 1986, this category leaped to 8.4 percent of all withdrawals by 1990, the third largest category of withdrawals behind housing and retirement in that year. With the introduction in 1993 of the Shares Top-Up and Enhanced Investment Schemes, withdrawals for investment exploded to 52.0 percent of all withdrawals during that year.

Next we can look at the more recent objectives of the CPF—health care and education. In health care, Medisave was a new program in 1985, and it accounted for only 1.3 percent of withdrawals during that year. By 1990 Medisave had grown in importance and had been joined by Medishield. Together these two health-related schemes accounted for 6.1 percent of withdrawals in 1990. It is noteworthy that increases in CPF health withdrawals moderated between 1990 and 1993, rising only about 21.7 percent in nominal dollars, and falling to 2.7 percent of total CPF withdrawals in 1993. Singapore is highly determined to keep health expenditures low and CPF withdrawals for health care reflect this policy emphasis.

Within CPF, the social objective of education is addressed only by the Education Scheme, which began in 1989. This scheme is restrictive, and only a portion of the population goes on to tertiary education in Singapore. Therefore, compared to most other uses of the CPF, withdrawals are rather small. In 1993 the Education Scheme accounted for only 0.2 percent of CPF withdrawals.

Also of interest is a CPF-like scheme called Edusave. In December 1990, Prime Minister Goh Chok Tong announced Edusave saying, "I want to give everybody a chance to appear at the same starting line, regardless of his financial background. . . . I have come up with the Edusave programme because I want to temper our meritocratic, free market system with compassion and more equal opportunities." (*Straits Times,* 18 December 1990). Mr. Goh had recently assumed the office of prime minister. He called Edusave "an investment in our children." Significantly, if the money is not used by completion of "O" level (the equivalent of high school), the balance goes into the CPF Ordinary Account. Thus, it seems quite possible that Edusave will be integrated into the CPF in the future.

Edusave is a major departure because virtually all young people will have accounts, which can later be transferred to a CPF Ordinary Account; and the government is making universal deposits that are not tied directly to employment. These are very important policy precedents. Although deposited amounts are currently modest, the Edusave structure opens the door to a truly universal CPF with multiple funding channels. In 1995 this potential became apparent as the government announced matching grants to community groups that raise money for Edusave accounts for children in their communities.

SINGAPOREANS' VIEWS ON THE CPF AND PATTERNS OF PARTICIPATION

There is not enough space here to present focus group and survey results in detail (see Sherraden, 1995 and Sherraden, et al., 1995), but we can present summary information. Overall, Singaporeans are very pleased with the CPF. The defined contribution nature of the CPF is highly valued, and social insurance is viewed as unfair and a fiscal disaster. This viewpoint is dominant across all segments and classes of Singaporeans, even those who would objectively be better off under a system of social insurance. Compulsory contributions are a popular feature of the CPF and the high contribution rate is endorsed by most Singaporeans, although many say that workers with low incomes should get some relief or subsidy. Singaporeans think that the CPF has very positive impacts on individuals, families, and the nation as a whole.

The CPF is viewed primarily as a savings and retirement scheme, even though the major use of funds to date has been for housing. This perception may indicate that even though most CPF resources are tied up in housing, these resources are still viewed by CPF members as security for retirement. The move toward reverse mortgages announced in January 1994 is consistent with this interpretation, allowing Singaporeans to use their housing assets without moving from the residence. Although most CPF assets are currently tied up in housing, this pattern may change in the future. Uses of the CPF are likely to shift as greater funds accumulate, the population ages, and home ownership increasingly occurs through intergenerational transfer.

Therefore, it remains important to ask Singaporeans what they intend to do with their lump-sum payments at retirement. Other than living expenses and health care, saving ranks very high, as does improving the personal residence. Other real property and share investments rank low, but human and social investments rank high. These human and social investments include helping the next generation and giving money to religious and voluntary organizations. The only significant consumption use (other than living expenses and health care) is travel at age fifty-five, which tends to be very popular in Singapore. Purchases of durable goods (furniture or car) are planned by relatively few members.

Turning to specific impacts, respondents give very high marks to the CPF across a broad range of economic, psychological, and social effects. Foremost, the CPF is viewed as an effective vehicle for providing housing and health care. A number of positive behavioral effects are also indicated, particularly in taking care of property, planning for the future, and working. Psychological effects of asset holding—greater confidence, increased security, a sense of control—are also noteworthy. Social effects are somewhat less prominent in stronger community relations and in not migrating from Singapore.

Several types of hypothesized effects do not receive much support. These include the limited impact on social attachments to voluntary and political organizations and the limited impact on family formation (getting married at earlier ages and having more children). Indeed, although we did not test this, it is possible that the CPF actually has a negative impact on family formation because of the greater opportunity cost (foregoing CPF accumulations) for women who interrupt employment for child rearing. However, when asked about the intergenerational effects of the CPF, the vast majority of respondents say that children are better off. From focus groups, we know that the reason is greater asset accumulation and the opportunities this will provide to the next generation.

Also ranking low in effects are all types of investments other than the personal residence. However, with the expansion of the CPF into the Enhanced Investment Scheme and the Shares Top-Up Scheme for Telecom shares (and presumably successor subsidized share schemes in future privatizations), it is likely that this pattern will be altered in the future. Senior

Minister Lee Kuan Yew and Prime Minister Goh Chok Tong have discussed the importance of asset building and stake holding. Following the success of home ownership, Singapore's leaders have announced share ownership as the next undertaking in asset accumulation across the population.

One might expect certain unfavorable effects of the CPF as well. As a theoretical matter, the greatest of these would be the consumption that is foregone by saving such a large percentage of income. Indeed, 38.5 percent of respondents say that making CPF contributions causes at least some financial difficulty. Discontent may also be suggested in the call for greater flexibility in use of funds. On the other hand, we find strong general support for investment as opposed to consumption in the use of CPF funds, both before and after age fifty-five. Regarding security, there is widespread concern about adequacy issues, especially as these relate to today's older population who have not accumulated large CPF balances, lower income working people, or those who are not working.

CONCLUSIONS

The Central Provident Fund is the primary domestic policy in Singapore. Its development, scope, and impact are impressive. Two summary observations on CPF policy change and impact may be in order. First, the CPF began as a simple provident fund for old age but expanded to new areas of social policy, including housing, transportation, health care, investments, and education. It has moved decidedly away from the basic provident fund concept of a single lump-sum payment at age fifty-five and has become a wide-ranging social security and economic development system. Second, stark individualism has been gradually moderated over the years, and the system is moving toward greater protection and more required safeguards (a back-up account, a forced annuity for retirement, intrafamily transfers, and insurances).

It is readily apparent that the CPF changes with social and economic conditions and that the general direction has been toward ever-increasing elaboration into new social and economic purposes via new schemes. These trends began with the Public Housing Scheme in 1968 and accelerated during the 1980s, a decade in which nine new schemes were introduced, aiming at multiple social objectives—housing, health care, investment, retirement security, family protection, education, and even company welfarism.

By international standards, this has been almost a whirlwind of public policy development. And there is every indication that it is continuing in the 1990s, with the introduction of Medishield in 1990, Edusave (not officially part of the CPF) in 1993, and the Shares Top-Up Scheme in 1993. What lies behind this rapid transformation of a simple provident fund into a domestic policy system with multiple facets? There are several possible answers to this question, but the key ones are an activist state that tends to construct as much domestic policy as possible around principles of individual asset accumulation rather than social insurance or need-based welfare payments, and the rapid accumulation of the CPF funds (due to a combination of high contribution rates and rising real earnings), which makes it possible for households to fund these new policy initiatives. The liberalization of the use of the funds has led to the rise of a middle-class, asset-owning society that has enhanced social and political stability. In particular, if not for the CPF, there would be a much smaller middle class of homeowners.

With the CPF's multiple purposes and expanding system, one other key point should be noted. Because all of this policy occurs within a single system of individual accounts operated through one governmental body, albeit in coordination with many others, a degree of integration occurs, at both micro and macro levels, that is unknown in the complex social policies of most countries. The CPF system effectively avoids overlapping bureaucracies and puts many domestic matters "on the same table" for decisions regarding policy development, as well as for decisions by members on the use of funds. Some may argue that this system centralizes too much power and influence in one place. However, it is a centralization that has huge benefits in rational planning and efficiency of operation, and it simultaneously places considerable choice in the hands of individual members. The key to this seeming contradiction—centralized planning yet greater individual choice—is a domestic policy system based on asset accumulation at the individual level.

Social Impacts

By far the most important social impact of the CPF to date has been in housing. As Senior Minister Lee Kuan Yew said in an interview for this study, the decision in 1968 to use CPF funds to promote home ownership was intended to help Singaporeans identify with the nation and to fight for the country should that become necessary. There is little doubt that widespread home ownership has had a major impact on social stability. Assets in housing have enabled most Singaporeans, even those with low incomes, to become stakeholders. The positive psychological impact of the CPF is also noteworthy. Confidence, security, control, and independence rank high as effects of the CPF. We know from focus group discussion that Singaporeans feel empowered by the CPF. In a sense, their social policy decisions are in their hands and they generally like it that way. However, there is concern among those who have very small CPF balances, who doubt that it will be enough.

There is a question about the impact of the CPF on family formation and childbearing. It is noteworthy that "have more children" ranks at the bottom of the list of possible effects of CPF participation and also at the bottom of the list of possible effects of home ownership. Most Singaporeans do not see any connection between the CPF and decisions to bear children. Indeed, there is nothing in the structure of the CPF that promotes childbearing. Moreover, the added economic incentive of the CPF probably makes some women reluctant to leave the work force to bear and raise children. Given Singapore's low birthrate, this may be a matter of concern to policy makers.

As we look to the future, the next generation of Singaporeans will inherit substantial wealth in homes, shares, and CPF cash balances. It is likely that CPF schemes will continue to expand as these resources grow, coverage and adequacy will continue to improve, and social impacts will become even more pronounced and more varied than in the past.

Authoritarian Government, Innovation, and Rapid Policy Development

The Singapore government exercises a degree of control over public and personal matters that is extreme by Western standards. It is important to bear in mind, however, that the political regime is highly popular. Singaporeans are in general happy with the current political arrangement, in large part because the government has delivered both rapid economic growth and social order. The CPF is a key part of Singapore's economic prosperity and social stability.

In many respects, the CPF exemplifies the nature of Singapore's government. Above all else, the government is practical. The orientation is to solve problems, actual or anticipated, rather than to maintain allegiance to any particular ideology or policy structure. The emphasis on practicality and problem solving is reflected in the innovative and rapid policy development within the CPF. The government's control makes it possible to shift directions rather quickly, and the government uses the simple CPF policy structure for multiple and growing applications. As capital accumulates in the CPF, this trend is likely to continue into the future.

Successes and Concerns

In many respects the CPF has been quite successful: multiple policy purposes are integrated into a single system; bureaucracy is kept to a minimum; participants feel empowered by having CPF accounts; the CPF is very popular; the vast majority of Singaporeans have become homeowners; Medisave has helped to contain health-care costs; the CPF is now being channeled into widespread share ownership; and a great deal of capital has accumulated, which in turn has had very positive macroeconomic effects.

In other ways, the CPF is not so successful. Foremost, there are concerns about coverage of the population and adequacy of funds for retirement security. Many older Singaporeans have little invested in the CPF and back-up assistance programs are very limited. However, regarding adequacy and coverage, two trends are encouraging. First, increasing capital in CPF accounts is gradually reducing problems of adequacy. Most younger workers will be in much better shape than the older cohorts now retiring. Also, the next generation of Singaporeans will inherit substantial wealth in homes, shares, and CPF cash balances, which will add to their retirement security. Second, there are signs of expansion in coverage. The long-term intention is to bring the self-employed fully into the CPF. The introduction of Edusave and the Shares Top-Up Scheme are very important as policy precedents because accounts are made available to Singaporeans who are not working and money is being put into accounts by the government that is not tied to work behavior. These precedents, though small, offer the possibility of universal coverage at some point in the future.

An Observation on Savings, Culture, and Institutions

It is common for academics and other observers, in Singapore and elsewhere, to explain high savings rates in East and Southeast Asia in terms of cultural characteristics, usually invoking the theme of Confucian values. But the modern history of Singapore and the CPF suggests that culture has little to do with Singapore's high savings rate. When the current government took over in 1959, the savings rate was actually negative (one government official decried in Parliament that the Chinese never save); yet in 1991 the Singapore savings rate was 48 percent of GDP, the highest in the world. This change in savings rate occurred with a population that remained largely the same during this period. Thus culture is a very inadequate explanation. Nor are neoclassical views of individuals' propensity to accumulate a satisfactory explanation for saving in Singapore.

A far better explanation is institutional: saving in Singapore is above all else a function of government policy. This is rather easy to demonstrate. The Singapore government itself accounts for about half of gross national savings (GNS). In the household sector, the CPF accounts for an additional 25 percent of GNS (1991 figures). Note that the CPF has very little to do with group culture or an individual's propensity to accumulate. Instead, the CPF is structured, subsidized, and facilitated by public policy.

Asset-Based Policy in Western Welfare States

Welfare states are characterized by the transfer of income to support consumption. Social insurance and means-tested transfers make up well over half of most government budgets in the West. In this social policy scheme, an individual's "welfare" (well-being) is defined by his or her level of income, and it is assumed that this income supports a certain level of consumption. This definition of welfare-as-consumption derives from faulty intellectual underpinnings in the neoclassical theory that has shaped welfare economics. As any ordinary accountant or financial planner knows, consumption by itself does not constitute well-being. Savings and investment—asset building—must be taken into consideration as well. Sherraden (1991) suggests that assets yield a number of important welfare effects in addition to deferred consumption.

The Central Provident Fund offers a policy model that is based on assumptions quite different from those employed in Western welfare states. The CPF recognizes that individuals, families, and the nation as a whole must balance income and consumption with savings and investment. Asset building is the foundation of domestic policy, so that many social and economic goals—especially home ownership, retirement security, and even health care—are achieved to a significant extent through asset accumulation.

By Western welfare state standards, the CPF can be criticized for being too extreme in its emphasis on asset accumulation, with not enough income and other supports to meet the basic needs of the very poor, the elderly who are alone, spouses who have not worked, or the migrant populations that make up a significant portion of the lower-tier labor force. From this perspective, a nation as wealthy as Singapore should be doing more to take care of the basic living conditions of the poorest who live within its borders. If we think simplistically of social policy as being a combination of income-based and asset-based strategies, Singapore may be out of balance, favoring assets.

On the other hand, Western welfare states are clearly out of balance, favoring income. As most leaders in Western Europe and North America are beginning to realize, the large-scale income-based policies that were created in the twentieth century are probably not sustainable over the long term. Changes will have to occur. It is likely that these national leaders will with great difficulty seek to balance income-based policies with asset-based policies. The key idea is balance—balancing social protections with individual asset accumulation. The challenge will always be to find the balance that is appropriate for a particular nation and its circumstances.

NOTE

Because Singapore is in some respects a challenging venue for social research by an outsider, a few research notes may be in order. I organized the study beginning with a visit to Singapore early in 1991. Following an invited speech to the Central Provident Fund Board and discussions with CPF managers and staff, I suggested a comprehensive study of the CPF. There was interest on the part of the board, but conditions were suggested that would make independent research impossible, including the editing of research reports by the board. I replied that it would not be possible to work under those conditions, but I would like to carry out the project if I were in full control. After my return to the United States and several months of silence, the board responded that the study could proceed; the board would cooperate in certain ways but would neither support the project financially nor direct it in any way. This was, from my perspective, an ideal arrangement, and I think it has worked out well for everyone involved.

Funding was pieced together from the Council for International Exchange of Scholars (Fulbright Research Fellowship), Washington University (research leave for Michael Sherraden), the University of Missouri at St. Louis (research leave for Margaret Sherrard Sherraden), the National University of Singapore (focus group and survey expenses), the Rockefeller Foundation (analysis and writing expenses), and the Dennis Trading Group (distribution of the research report).

The study began in the United States in 1991 with the work of Sudha Nair, a Singaporean research assistant. We were in Singapore from August 1992 through August 1993, devoting full time to data collection. The research project was housed at the National University of Singapore, and two NUS colleagues joined the research team, Dr. S. Vasoo and Dr. Ngiam Tee Liang. Additional analysis occurred during 1994 and 1996 and was aided by two assistants at Washington University, Deborah Page-Adams and Cheng Li-Chen.

CPF Board officials were cooperative throughout. They did everything that they said they would do. The librarian of the board was particularly helpful with documentary materials. Other government officials were also cooperative. Interviews were conducted with many leaders, including Senior Minister Lee Kuan Yew and leading economist Dr. Goh Keng Swee, who were principal architects of CPF policy over many years. We recruited members for focus groups as we thought best. I randomly selected the survey sample and the research team went into people's homes all over the country. No Singaporean attempted in any way to curtail research activities.

REFERENCES

Asher, Mukul G. (1983) Economic effects of the CPF scheme. *Singapore Business Yearbook*, 25–35.

Asher, Mukul G. (1991) *Social adequacy and equity of the social security arrangements in Singapore.* Occasional paper no. 8. Singapore: Centre for Advanced Studies, National University of Singapore.

Asher, Mukul G. (1992) *Financing social security through the National Provident Fund: The case of Singapore.* Paper prepared for the World Bank, National University of Singapore.

Central Provident Fund Board (1955–1992) *Annual reports.* Singapore: Central Provident Fund Board.

Central Provident Fund Study Group, National University of Singapore (1986) *Report of the Central Provident Fund Study Group.* In a special issue of *The Singapore Economic Review* 31(1).

Cheung, Paul (1992) Population ageing in Singapore. Paper presented at the WHO-MOH joint workshop on healthy ageing, Singapore, October.

Chow, N.W.S. (1981) Social security provision in Singapore and Hong Kong. *Journal of Social Policy* 10(3); 353–56.

Chua Beng Huat (1988) Public housing policies compared: U.S., socialist countries, and Singapore. Paper presented at the 83rd annual meeting of the American Sociological Association, Atlanta.

Deutsch, Antal and Hanna Zowall (1988) *Compulsory savings and taxes in Singapore.* Singapore: Institute of Southeast Asian Studies.

Dixon, John (1989a) Social security traditions and their global context. In *Glimpses of international and comparative social welfare,* ed. Brij Mohan. Canberra: International Fellowship for Social and Economic Development.

Dixon, John (1989b) A comparative perspective on provident funds: Their present and future explained. *Journal of International and Comparative Social Welfare* 5(2); 1–28.

Dixon, John (1989c) *National provident funds: The enfant terrible of social security.* Canberra: International Fellowship for Social and Economic Development.

Friedman, Barry L. (1989) *A comparison of a provident fund and other pension systems.* Paper prepared for the State Commission for Restructuring the Economic System, Beijing, China, unpublished.

Goh Keng Swee (1956) *Urban incomes and housing: A report of the social survey of Singapore,* 1953–54. Singapore: Government Printer.

Goh Keng Swee (1977) *The practice of economic growth.* Singapore: Federal Publications.

Goh, Lee E. (1988) Planning that works: Housing policy and economic development in Singapore. *Journal of Planning Education and Research* 7(3);147–62.

Iau, Robert (1979) The CPF: Its objectives and operations. Singapore: Inland Revenue Department.

International Social Security Association [ISSA] (1962) *First regional meeting for Asia and Oceania.* Report on meeting held in Tokyo. Geneva: ISSA.

International Social Security Association, Regional Office for Asia and the Pacific (1965) *Main features of Asian provident funds.* Second regional conference for Asia and Oceania. New Delhi: ISSA Regional Office.

International Social Security Association, Committee on Provident Funds (publication beginning 1975) *Reports of meetings of the committee.* Geneva: ISSA.

Jones, Catherine (1990) Hong Kong, Singapore, South Korea, and Taiwan: Oikonomic welfare states. *Government and Opposition* 25, 446–62.

Kalirajan, K. and Paitoon Wiboonchutikula (1986) The social security system in Singapore. In Tyabji, ed., 129–39.

Krause, Lawrence B., Koh Ai Tee, and Lee (Tsao) Yuan (1987) *The Singapore economy reconsidered.* Singapore: Institute of Southeast Asian Studies.

Liew Kian Siong (1992) *The state of welfare in Singapore.* M.S.S. thesis, Department of Sociology, National University of Singapore.

Lim Chong Yah (1988) *Policy options for the Singapore economy.* New York: McGraw-Hill.

Lim, Linda Y. C. (1989) Social welfare. In Sandhu and Wheatly, 171–97.

Phau Kai Hong (1991) *Privitisation and restructuring of health services in Singapore.* Occasional paper no. 5. Singapore: Institute for Policy Studies.

Pugh, Cedric (1984) Public policy, welfare and the Singapore economy. *Annales de L'Economia Publique Sociale et Cooperative*, no. 4, 433–55.

Pugh, Cedric (1987) Housing in Singapore: The effective ways of the unorthodox. *Environment and Behavior* 19(3); 311–30.

Queisser, Monika (1991) Social security schemes in South-East Asia. *International Social Security Review* 44(1/2); 121–35.

Republic of Singapore (1989) *Report of the Advisory Committee on the Aged.* Singapore: Government Printer.

Republic of Singapore (1992) *Towards better health care: Report of the Health Care Review Committee.* Singapore: Government Printer.

Republic of Singapore, Ministry of Health (1984) *Report of the Committee on the Problems of the Aged* ("Howe Report"). Singapore: Government Printer.

Sandhu, K. S. and Paul Wheatly, eds. (1989) *The management of success: The moulding of modern Singapore.* Singapore: Institute of Southeast Asian Studies.

Sherraden, Michael (1991). *Assets and the poor: A new American welfare policy.* Armonk, NY: M.E. Sharpe.

Sherraden, Michael (1995) Social policy based on assets: Singapore's Central Provident Fund. Paper presented at the Annual Meeting of the Association for Asian Studies, Washington, April.

Sherraden, Michael, Sudha Nair, S. Vasoo, Ngiam Tee Liang and Margaret S. Sherraden (1995) Social policy based on assets: The impact of Singapore's Central Provident Fund. *Asian Journal of Political Science* 3(2); 112–133.

Shome, Parthasarrathi and Kathrine Anderson Saito (1985) *Social security institutions and capital creation: Singapore, the Philippines, Malaysia, India and Sri Lanka.* Kuala Lumpur: Sritua Arief Associates.

Tan, Augustine H. H. and Phang Sock-Yong (1991) *The Singapore experience in public housing.* Occasional paper no. 9. Centre for Advanced Studies, National University of Singapore. Singapore: Times Academic Press.

Toh Mun Heng and Linda Low (1991) *Health care economics, policies and issues in Singapore.* Centre for Advanced Studies, National University of Singapore. Singapore: Times Academic Press.

Tracy, Martin, reporting for the Committee on Provident Funds (1992) *Experience of provident funds in the provision of housing and scope for improvement.* A report at the Fourteenth General Assembly. Geneva: International Social Security Association.

Tyabji, Amina (1990) Financing social security. Paper presented at a conference on the Fiscal System in Singapore, National University of Singapore, February.

Tyabji, Amina, ed. (1986) *Social security systems in ASEAN.* Special edition of *ASEAN Economic Bulletin* 3(1).

U.S. Department of Health and Human Services, Social Security Administration (1990) *Social security programs throughout the world, 1989.* Washington: U.S. Government Printing Office.

Wee Chow Hou and Han Sin Bee (1983) The Central Provident Fund—Some micro and macro issues. *Singapore Management Review* 5(2); 35–52.

Wong, Aline and Stephen H. K. Yeh, eds. (1985) *Housing a nation: Twenty five years of public housing in Singapore.* Singapore: Maruzen Asia for the Housing Development Board.

Yee, Lionel D. (1991) Problems and issues faced by provident fund schemes in Asia and the Pacific. *Asian News Sheet* (International Social Security Association) 21(2); 24–28.

Yeh, Stephen H. K., ed. (1975) *Public housing in Singapore.* Singapore: Singapore University Press.

4

Noncontributory Pensions in Hong Kong: An Alternative to Social Security?

K. L. Tang

Social security is a major instrument for the relief of poverty in all advanced industrial countries. There are, however, different types of social security programs. Social insurance is the most favored approach, followed by social assistance. On the other hand, noncontributory social allowances such as child benefits, retirement pensions or universal housing subsidies are much less popular (Midgley, 1984; Hill and Bramley, 1986; Dixon, 1993). These provisions involve transfers without either contributions or means tests to particular categories of people. They are funded from general taxation and may be regarded as a subsidy paid by the state to assist people who have special needs. It is important to stress that income is not taken into account in determining eligibility. Social allowances are also known as demogrants because they provide social security to particular demographic groups, such as the elderly, children, and those with physical disabilities.

This approach to social security has a long history. Chancellor Bismarck's social insurance proposals in Germany were influenced by the French system of demogrants for industrial workers in the 1850s. The "pre-social insurance" British old-age pension scheme of 1908 offered assistance to respectable, aged poor who were too proud to apply for poor relief (Jones, 1990). Sweden's *folkpension*, which was introduced in 1946, was a universal noncontributory scheme (Williamson and Pampel, 1993). The demogrant has also been raised in discussions on social security reform in Britain. Seeking to "move on from Beveridge" and away from insurance principles, there have been calls for benefits as of right that are universally available and funded out of general taxation (Hill and Bramley, 1986).

However, financial pressure in the Western industrial nations has forced them to re-examine the role of universal social allowance programs. To a large extent, this assessment of universalism has been prompted by the challenge from the Radical Right, which has popularized the idea that state-sponsored welfare is inimical to economic and social progress. Adverse economic conditions and the collapse of postwar political consensus over the welfare state has also shaken welfare institutions in the United States and Britain (Midgley, 1991). Today many industrial countries are reviewing the role of universal social programs in their social welfare systems. In Sweden the Social Democratic party has been forced to pare back social welfare spending, and it has recently proposed to reduce the child allowance. In Canada the Conservative federal government introduced the Child Tax Benefit to replace the Family Allowance in 1993 (Axsworthy Report, 1994).

In view of these developments, the demogrant option seems to be of little potential value as an alternative to conventional social insurance programs. In this respect, Hong Kong's noncontributory, social allowance old-age pension is worth examining. There is a general consensus that the system, in existence for the last twenty years, is working well. Indeed, many social security experts believe that it is indispensable. In the following section I examine Hong Kong's social allowance scheme in light of the colony's political and socioeconomic development and consider its viability as an alternative form of social security.

HONG KONG AND ITS SOCIAL SECURITY SYSTEM

Hong Kong is presently a colony under British rule and it will remain so until 1997 when it reverts to China. Over 98 percent of its 6.2 million inhabitants are Chinese. Hong Kong was acquired as a part of the settlement imposed on China in 1842 after Britain's victory in the First Opium War. Victory in the Second Opium War of 1858–1860 forced the Qing dynasty to grant further concessions, including the permanent cession of the Kowloon Peninsula (opposite Hong Kong Island) to Britain. Finally, in 1898 Britain obtained by pressure the lease of the New Territories (lands adjacent to the Kowloon peninsula) for ninety-nine years. The national humiliation of these unequal treaties was keenly felt by most Chinese. This explains in large part the frequent demands on the part of later Chinese governments for the return of Hong Kong (Scott, 1989;

Miners, 1993). Under the terms of the Joint Declaration of 1985 between the British government and the communist regime in China, Hong Kong will become a Special Administrative Region of the People's Republic of China in 1997.

Hong Kong is ruled by a governor, who is appointed by the Queen. The governor has full authority over the colony's administration. Until recently, there was no elected legislature and the sole form of representation consisted of an appointed Executive Council. In response to a growing clamor for democratic involvement, the British introduced limited electoral representation in 1986. The first full and direct elections were held in 1991. Since then, Britain has sought to introduce a more representative structure in order to speed up democratic development. However, there has been strong opposition from China, which is very suspicious of these developments.

Under British rule, the colony has developed into a prosperous and capitalistic metropolis. The economy has grown very rapidly. In the 1970s, annual gross domestic product growth averaged 9.2 percent while the average growth rate in the 1980s has been 7.5 percent (Tsang, 1994). In 1993, the gross domestic product grew by 5.5 percent in real terms. Economic growth in Hong Kong has almost eliminated open unemployment. The unemployment rate was 2 percent and the underemployment rate was 1.5 percent in 1993 (Hong Kong, 1994a). The economic outlook for Hong Kong remains rosy. In his recent budget speech, the colony's financial secretary predicted gross domestic growth of 5.5 percent for the fiscal year 1994–1995, with per capita gross domestic product rising to $20,600, which is higher than that of either Britain or Australia (*Far Eastern Economic Review*, 17 March 1994).

Since the 1980s, the colony has moved from the stage of export-oriented industrialization based on the export of traditional light, labor-intensive manufactured products to a more complex and sophisticated level of export-oriented industrialization based on the export of more capital and technology-intensive manufactured products. At the same time, Hong Kong has continued to grow into a major international services and financial center.

The British administration in Hong Kong remains committed to a laissez-faire economic doctrine. The government believes that the allocation of resources in the economy is best left to market forces, with minimal government intervention in the private sector. The government further contends that the colony's free enterprise, market-disciplined system has contributed to its economic success. The government maintains that a simple tax structure, with low tax rates, provides a good incentive for workers to work and for entrepreneurs to invest. The primary role of government is to provide the necessary infrastructure and a sound legal and administrative framework conducive to economic growth and prosperity. The government believes in trickle-down economics, maintaining that economic success will eventually benefit all classes of people. It has adopted a hands-off approach in the economic sphere and resisted calls for social planning. It takes pride in the fact that industrial wages have doubled, that exports have grown by an average of 13.8 percent each year, and the proportion of households in acute poverty has shrunk to 16 percent from more than 50 percent.

The espousal of a free market, capitalist approach to development has been accompanied by an official disdain for the welfare state (Hodge, 1980b). Many Asian governments share this sentiment and this attitude is shared by the business community. Many believe that Asia's economic success is due to the absence of extensive welfare programs that, they contend, have sapped the economic energy of European countries. Although these views are frequently expressed, few seem to recognize that many Asian countries, including Hong Kong, have also introduced social programs of a great variety (Midgley, 1986). Hong Kong's social allowance scheme, which provides benefits to all elderly persons irrespective of their income, is one program of this kind.

Social Security Programs in Hong Kong

Prior to 1971, social welfare in Hong Kong was largely confined to the provision of temporary relief to the destitute and needy. The government restricted its role and stressed the role of the family in social welfare. In its first *White Paper on Social Welfare*, published in 1965, the government argued that the family should be strengthened so that it could provide adequate support and help to its members (Hong Kong, 1965). Compared to other social services, such as public housing, social welfare has developed more slowly. The Social Welfare Department came into existence only in 1958 (Heppell, 1973). In the early 1970s, more attention was given to social planning. Long-term plans in social welfare (public assistance and social allowance) were introduced. Public spending as a proportion of gross domestic product went up from around 13 percent during the decade of the 1960s to an average of 16 percent over the 1973–1978 period. Social spending per capita doubled between 1971 and 1974 (Tang, 1996).

The foundation of Hong Kong's social security system is the public assistance scheme. Public assistance (now known as the Comprehensive Social Security Assistance Scheme) was introduced in 1971. Its introduction indicated the willingness of the government to take care of the basic needs of those who are infirm and ill. Since then, this system has served as a safety net for the poor. Being means-tested, it provides cash assistance (together with a rent subsidy and special grants) to those in need, and it is designed to raise the income of needy individuals and families to a level where essential requirements of subsistence are met. The majority of recipients are the elderly, the disabled, and single parent families. The social assistance scheme has not changed significantly since its introduction in 1971 (MacPherson, 1993).

In 1973 the social allowance scheme (now known as Social Security Allowance Scheme) was introduced. Together with public assistance, it forms the mainstay of social security in Hong Kong. In the last twenty years, the government has relied heavily on these two schemes to deal with the financial problems of the poor, the infirm, and the aged. In addition, it has until recently refused to expand the social security system through the introduction of social insurance.

Although the Comprehensive Social Security Assistance Scheme and the Social Security Allowance Scheme are the major components of the colony's social security system, they are supplemented by three other schemes: the Criminal and Law Enforcement Injuries Compensation Scheme, the Traffic Accident Victims Assistance Scheme, and Emergency Relief. All these schemes are financed out of general taxation. The administration of these social security schemes is the responsibility of the Social Welfare Department. Total spending on social welfare in 1993 and 1994 amounted to HK $7,963 million (US $1,020 million). Of this amount, about HK $2,074 million (US $265 million) was spent on social assistance, while HK $3,052 million (US $391 million) was spent on the social allowance scheme. Social security spending comprises about 65 percent of total social welfare spending.

Throughout the 1980s, social welfare spending has fluctuated between 4.5 percent and 6.5 percent of the government's budget. Social security spending amounts to about 0.57 percent of the gross domestic product, compared with 0.44 percent in 1981. The increase in social security spending is mainly accounted for by the growing number of elderly persons receiving the old-age allowance (Chow, 1990). The government was alarmed early by the surge in old-age allowance spending. In 1976 the financial secretary expressed concern over this expansion. However, the scheme has not only survived but grown. Still, the cost of the scheme continues to be an issue. The old-age allowance scheme is estimated to cost as much as a third of the entire welfare budget.

HONG KONG'S SOCIAL SECURITY ALLOWANCE SCHEME

The social allowance scheme was first introduced in April of 1973. It provides a flat-rate, nonmeans-tested, and noncontributory cash benefit for the elderly and the severely disabled. It was initially called the Disability and Infirmity Allowance Scheme but was renamed the Special Needs Allowance Scheme in 1979. On July 1, 1993 it was renamed the Social Security Allowance Scheme. When the scheme was first introduced, the old-age allowance was confined to those who were over age seventy-five. In the late 1970s, this limit was lowered to cover those aged seventy or more. After 1988, the allowance was bifurcated: a higher old age allowance is now paid to those who are over seventy while those aged sixty-five to sixty-nine get a lower benefit. The allowance paid to those between the age of sixty-five and sixty-nine is, however, means tested.

To be eligible for an old-age allowance, a person must have resided in Hong Kong for at least five years after attaining the age of sixty. The old-age allowance is nonmeans-tested for those aged seventy and above and the recipients are entitled to HK $510 (US $65) per month. For those aged sixty-five to sixty-nine, the monthly allowance is set at HK $450 (US $59), subject to a declaration that income and assets do not exceed the prescribed levels. The income ceiling is HK $1,500 (US $192) per month for a single person and HK $2,500 (US $320) for a couple. The assets ceiling is much more generous. While the public assistance allowance accounts for some 15 percent of the median income, the social allowance constitutes some 7.7 percent to 8.8 percent of median income in 1991 (Social Security Society, 1991).

The number of people receiving disability and old-age allowances in 1994 was 466,399. Of these, it is estimated that about 60,000 are disabled persons who are not elderly (Hong Kong, 1994a). The expenditure on social security during the year was HK $3,051.9 million (US $391 million), representing an increase of 6.7 percent over the previous year. The increase in persons receiving the old-age allowance has been remarkable. In 1973 only 34,963 people were in the program. In 1979 the number increased to 143,669 recipients. In twenty years, there has been a sevenfold increase in the number of recipients.

The Philosophy of the Program

Although the social allowance program does not assess income as a criterion for granting an allowance, its implementation has been of immense help to those elderly poor who are receiving public assistance (Chow, 1984). But it is not designed to meet the subsistence needs of the elderly. Rather, it is a subsidy, intended to provide compensation to those with additional needs due to disability or old age. As such, it is regarded by some social policy writers as the epitome of a collectivist, social welfare provision (Midgley, 1984).

However, the introduction and expansion of social allowances in Hong Kong does not mean that the government is welfare minded. In fact, there has been an incrementalist stance on the part of government, which favors the gradual expansion of the existing program. The expansion of the program must also be seen in light of the government's overall social philosophy. Hodge (1980a) has identified three characteristics of Hong

Kong's social welfare system. First, he points out that any assessment of the colony's social welfare policy will recognize the absence of clearly defined social goals. Second, this reluctance to shape social policy to attain specific social goals is to be understood in the context of the economic uncertainties the colony has faced. The dominant public policy issue has been to insure that the colony remains fiscally viable. Thus, social welfare development has been largely determined by the availability of resources. Third, the government has ignored calls for a more equitable distribution of wealth through a higher level of taxation and increased social spending for fear that this will negatively affect the colony's economic development. This has also been a significant factor in social welfare policy.

Thus, while the government has been willing to provide a safety net for those least able to help themselves, it has been reluctant to expand welfare programs. It has been particularly careful to distance itself from the idea that it is creating a European-style welfare state (Hong Kong, 1991).

The Effectiveness of the Scheme

Hong Kong compares favorably with some advanced industrial countries, such as Sweden, Canada, and Japan, which also have demogrant social security programs. But what is peculiar about Hong Kong is that its noncontributory pension was introduced not in the wake of social insurance, as has been the case in many other countries, but as a substitute for it. Social allowances were introduced in Hong Kong as an improvement on public assistance (Jones, 1990). In this sense, Hong Kong may be viewed as having skipped a stage of development. The colony's social allowance scheme has provided additional resources for the aged poor who have found public assistance to be inadequate.

Initially the government believed that the scheme would be extended to other groups, such as widowed mothers with young children and the chronically ill. However, this never transpired due to the scheme's financial burden. It may be paradoxical, therefore, that the government lowered the age of eligibility from seventy-five to seventy years in 1977 and in so doing increased take-up and costs. This development reflects the government's adherence to an incrementalist style of social policy development. The change happened at a time when the government decided against welfare expansion in other fields (McLaughlin, 1993). A later reduction in the age of eligibility from seventy to sixty-five years was introduced in 1991 after the government turned down a proposal to establish a central provident fund. Critics have suggested that its willingness to lower the age of eligibility was an attempt to defuse support for a contributory social insurance scheme and represents a concession on the part of government.

An assessment of the effectiveness of the scheme must recognize that the allowance is not adequate to support the subsistence needs of recipients. The scheme is not designed to to provide relief to the poor. Instead, as was noted earlier, the allowance is a small subsidy signifying the government's willingness to acknowledge that elderly people have extra needs. Poor elderly people must still resort to public assistance for further help. While the allowance is insufficient to meet the needs of the elderly, it symbolizes societal care that is compatible with the traditional respect for the elderly in the Chinese community. This is confirmed in the survey of young people's views toward the old-age pension scheme. Of the respondents, 45 percent adhere strongly to the traditional belief that taking care of the elderly is a family responsibility (Federation of Youth Groups, 1994).

Although the scheme pays very small benefits, it has been well received by the elderly. The take-up rate is extremely high. MacPherson (1993) noted a 92 percent take-up rate for the social allowance, which is very effective at reaching its intended beneficiaries. In addition, its administrative costs are very low. There is no means test and monthly payments are made directly to the bank accounts of recipients. The Hong Kong experience has shown that social allowances are very easy to administer.

Another factor is the cost of the scheme. As has been noted already, substantial financial resources, obtained from general taxation, have been put into the scheme. The financial burden has also increased as many more elderly people have obtained benefits. This has prompted considerable discussion. Some commentators have asserted that it is not worth allocating sizable revenues that result in the payment of small benefits to a large number of beneficiaries. It would, they contend, be more cost-effective to impose a means test on all recipients, reduce the number of beneficiaries, and pay larger benefits to those who are truly in financial need.

On the other hand, some commentators have argued that the scheme should be expanded to cover all elderly persons over the age of sixty years. They believe that the scheme makes a significant contribution to the welfare of the elderly and exemplifies society's commitment to recognize and care for its elderly citizens.

Yet others believe that the social allowance scheme should be replaced with a contributory social insurance system to support the elderly upon retirement. An insurance approach, they assert, is the most desirable since it would be largely self-financed, comprehensive, and effective.

Discussion of these issues has gained momentum in recent years, and there has been considerable support among social policy experts for the introduction of a comprehensive insurance-funded retirement system. Although the government has consistently avoided undertaking a major overhaul of the social security system (Chow, 1990), it has in recent years been willing to consider the introduction of a social insurance scheme.

In 1993 it published proposals for a scheme of this kind. Since the possible introduction of a social insurance scheme would have a major impact on the current social allowance pension, it is necessary that these developments be considered in more detail.

THE SOCIAL INSURANCE OPTION

Calls for the introduction of a statutory, contributory old-age pension scheme were first made in the early 1970s, but these were unheeded. In the early 1980s, proposals for a semivoluntary social insurance scheme were formulated, but these too were formally rejected by the government. Since then, labor unions, social workers, and policy analysts have made concerted efforts to re-open the issue. Backed by various opinion polls that reveal the public's receptiveness to the introduction of a contributory scheme, advocates suggested that a provident fund be created. The proposal was also rejected by the government on two occasions, first in 1987 and then in 1991.

However, the pension issue could not be put off indefinitely. One factor is Hong Kong's fast-aging population. The proportion of people aged sixty and above is expected to grow from the current 13 percent of the population to 16 percent by 2006 (Tsang, 1991). In addition, Mok (1994) reported that the rate of impoverishment of the elderly exceeded 40 percent. One third of the elderly work up to age seventy and one tenth up to age eighty. Many elderly have to continue to work to earn a living. An earlier study by the labour unions revealed that half of the old people over sixty in Hong Kong have to work to support themselves and their families (Chan, 1992). Another issue has been Hong Kong's inadequate occupational pension arrangement for its 2.8 million-person work force. Only 30 percent of the work force is covered by corporate pension funds. Another 5 percent are civil servants, protected by government pension plans. The remainder of the work force is unprotected, except for the social assistance and social allowance scheme.

Sensing that pressure for some form of retirement protection was building, the government introduced in 1992 a proposal for a compulsory private provident fund scheme. This scheme was entitled the Retirement Protection Scheme. However, it was not favored by the business sector and grass-roots organizations since the private financial institutions that would run the program could, it was alleged, be financially vulnerable and savings could be lost, leaving workers without support (Mok, 1994).

Despite the fact that the government had previously been unwilling to act on social insurance, in 1993 it published proposals for a generous contributory old-age pension scheme that would retain some of the features of the demogrant social allowance scheme. The proposed scheme would provide HK $1,200 (US $150) a month (about a third of the local median wage) to anyone aged sixty-five or above, including housewives, the disabled, and the current elderly population. The money would come from current wage earners, who would have to pay up to 3 percent of their income to the scheme. Employers would contribute a similar amount. The present social allowance scheme would be abolished and the resources currently allocated to it would be re-allocated to the new pension plan. Although the scheme will be funded on a pay-as-you go basis by a payroll tax, it would cover all persons over the age of sixty-five irrespective of whether or not they had contributed to the scheme. The government asserts that its proposed scheme is fair and comprehensive and would be simple to administer. It further argues that it is a more effective approach than that of a central provident fund since it can be initiated immediately and would cover all elderly people.

Initial responses indicate strong support for the scheme. Those in favor include old people, social workers, labor unions, women's groups, professional bodies, and major political parties. On the other hand, some economists and business leaders oppose the plan on the grounds that the payroll tax will harm the economy. The first opinion poll on the proposal revealed that a majority of respondents supported the idea of a contributory old-age pension scheme (Mok, 1994). The government revealed that about 70 percent of the submissions it received from the public during the consultation period were also in favor of the plan. A survey of young people produced more mixed results. More were in favor of a pension scheme actuarially based on their own contributions. Young professionals with postsecondary education had the strongest reservations about the proposed scheme.

A major consideration in the debate on the introduction of social insurance concerns the transfer of sovereignty to China in 1997. Clearly, the Chinese government, which will inherit the scheme, will be a critically important party to the successful implementation of the proposals in the long run. Unfortunately, the Chinese government has been suspicious of the motives of the British administration in introducing plans that will extend beyond 1997. It is particularly wary of plans that will involve extra expenditures by the government. The Chinese are worried about the possibility that the British are going to exhaust all financial resources before their departure, leaving a fiscal wasteland behind them. Another concern on the part of the Chinese government is the likelihood that the British are seeking to create political and social tensions in the colony before they leave.

Suspicion and concern about the proposal are revealed in a response from the Chinese government to a speech made in 1994 by the governor of Hong Kong in which he promised increased social expenditures on education and services for the elderly. A senior Beijing official was quoted as complaining that excessive welfarism would pose a huge financial burden on Hong Kong after 1997. Another Chinese official has commented that plans to increase social welfare spending threaten to sap Hong Kong's "spirit of diligence" and turn the territory into a "welfare society." The communist government in China has also supported the concerns of the business community. If the business community and the Chinese administration collaborate, it is likely that the scheme will not be implemented.

These reactions from the Chinese government must be seen in the context of wider diplomatic relations between Britain and China. Relations between the two countries over the future of Hong Kong have been tense since 1992. China has angrily denounced the colony's democratization policies, which increased popular participation in the elections of members of the legislature. China has announced its intention to abolish the legislature after its assumes power.

It is unlikely that the proposal for social insurance will be implemented. Despite the fact that many ordinary people favor the scheme, many are reluctant to support the introduction of a new scheme just prior to the transfer of Hong Kong to Chinese rule. There is just too much uncertainty at present, and many believe that the issue will not be satisfactorily resolved until the transfer of power has taken place. Faced with opposition from the business community and Chinese authorities, the government announced in January of 1995 that it would not implement the plan. It also announced that it would not create a provident fund. It reiterated its earlier willingness to support the introduction of a compulsory private insurance plan, but it is unlikely that this proposal will be supported or that any significant policy changes will be introduced. Surprisingly, in mid-1995 the government reversed its earlier announcement that it would not support the introduction of a provident fund. However, after the legislative elections of 1995, the majority pro-democracy group renewed the campaign for social insurance. At the time of this writing, the likelihood that some form of contributory scheme will be introduced remains uncertain.

THE ROLE OF SOCIAL ALLOWANCES

Hong Kong has lost many opportunities to address the needs of the elderly. The recent proposal for a contributory, insurance-funded retirement scheme has come too late. Accordingly, the social allowance scheme is here to stay for the time being. It will either be retained or replaced by the Chinese government after the transition in power of 1997. On the other hand, it could be augmented. Given the fact that the current levels of benefits are small, it is preferable that the scheme be augmented by additional forms of protection, such as social insurance or social assistance. This recommendation was, in fact, supported by a group of international experts who came to Hong Kong in 1990 to study the colony's social security system. The group's conclusion was that the existing social allowance scheme should be kept intact but that it should be extended by an additional social insurance scheme (Social Security Society, 1991).

The experience of Hong Kong suggests that social allowances have an important role to play in a comprehensive social security system. They are highly effective as a supplement to social insurance and social assistance programs but are of limited value when they are used exclusively to cater to those in need. As was noted earlier, they do not pay sufficient benefits to raise incomes above subsistence levels, and they are generally costly. The cost factor is particularly relevant in societies in which populations are aging and in which economic adversity is a present reality. Obviously, an expanding economy is necessary for the survival of the demogrant approach. In conditions of economic adversity, there is a distinct possibility that these schemes will be trimmed.

The cost factor also makes the allowance approach politically vulnerable. In Hong Kong, some have argued that more resources should be devoted to the most needy sections of society rather than to the elderly as a demographic group. In Sweden, a similar argument arose when the *folkpension* was introduced in 1946. The Social Democratic Party was hesitant about a universal pension system since it feared that more resources would go to the middle class rather than to needy lower-income people.

Another problem is that the absence of a direct link between contributions and benefits also makes these schemes politically vulnerable. Unlike social insurance, which is perceived by the public to provide benefits as a result of contributions paid into the system over a lifetime of work, there is no such link in social allowances.

While these and other reasons suggest that a social security strategy based exclusively on social allowances is risky, the harmonization of this approach with other social security approaches is desirable. The social allowance approach subsidizes and compensates for the additional burdens faced by people in retirement, those with disabilities, and those with young children. As such they not only address additional needs, but foster solidarity and collective responsibility. They represent a common responsibility for all people while paying respect to the dignity of the individual. Despite the fact that these values are today increasingly neglected, they continue to have relevance for the future well-being of society.

REFERENCES

Axworthy Report (1994) *Improving social security in Canada: A discussion paper.* Ottawa: Human Resources Development.

Chan, Y. H. (1992) The urgency of establishing a comprehensive retirement scheme. *Welfare Digest* 211: 1–2.

Chow, N.W.S. (1984) *A critical study of social welfare policy in Hong Kong.* Hong Kong: Cosmo.

Chow, N.W.S. (1990) Social welfare. In *The other Hong Kong report*, eds. R. Young and J. Cheng. Hong Kong: Chinese University Press, 429–44.

Chui, S., Ngan, R.M.H., and J. Woo (1993) The production of inequality in social security provisions. In *Asia Regional Conference on Social Security, September 14–16, 1993*, Hong Kong Council of Social Services. Hong Kong: Hong Kong Council of Social Services, 255–69.

Dixon, J. (1993) Social security in the nineties: Challenges and prospects: Reflections on the connection between social security and poverty. In *Asia Regional Conference on Social Security, September 14–16, 1993*, Hong Kong Council of Social Services. Hong Kong: Hong Kong Council of Social Services, 3–27.

Heppell, T. S. (1973) Social security and social welfare: A new look from Hong Kong: Part One. *Journal of Social Policy* 2(3): 225–38.

Heppell, T. S. and P. R. Webb (1973) Planning social welfare: The Hong Kong experience. *International Social Work* 16(4): 16–25.

Hill, M. J. and G. Bramley (1986) *Analysing Social Policy*. Oxford: Blackwell.

Hodge, P. (1980a) Social planning models and their application in Hong Kong. In *Social welfare in Hong Kong*. Hong Kong: Council of Social Services, 1–22.

Hodge, P. (1980b) Expectations and dilemmas of social welfare in Hong Kong. In *Hong Kong dilemmas of growth*, eds. C. K. Leung, J. W. Cushman and G. Wang, Canberra: Australian National University Press, 465–94.

Hong Kong, Federation of Youth Groups (1994) *Young people's views on retirement benefits*. Hong Kong: Federation of Youth Groups.

Hong Kong (1965) *Aims and policy for social welfare in Hong Kong: White paper on social welfare*. Hong Kong: Government Printer.

Hong Kong (1973) *The way ahead: White paper on social welfare*. Hong Kong: Government Printer.

Hong Kong (1977) *Help for those least able to help themselves: A program of social security development: Green paper on social welfare*. Hong Kong: Government Printer.

Hong Kong (1979) *Social welfare into the 1980s*. Hong Kong: Government Printer.

Hong Kong (1991) *Social welfare into the 1990s*. Hong Kong: Government Printer.

Hong Kong (1992) *Hong Kong 1991 population census: Main tables*. Hong Kong: Census and Statistics Department.

Hong Kong (1994a) *Hong Kong annual report, 1994*. Hong Kong: Government Printer.

Hong Kong (1994b) *Hong Kong monthly digest of statistics*. Hong Kong: Government Printer.

Hong Kong (1994c) *Taking the worry out of growing old: A consultation paper on the government's proposals for an old age pension scheme*. Hong Kong: Government Printer.

Hong Kong Federation of Youth Groups (1994) *A study of young people's attitudes toward contributory old-age pension program*. Hong Kong: Hong Kong Federation of Youth Groups, Research Office.

Jones, C. (1990) *Promoting prosperity: The Hong Kong way of social policy*. Hong Kong: The Chinese University Press.

Lee, A.S.Y.C. (1993) Social security in Hong Kong. In *Asia Regional Conference on Social Security September 14–16, 1993*, Hong Kong Council of Social Services. Hong Kong: Hong Kong Council of Social Services, 158–168.

MacPherson, S. (1993) Social security in Hong Kong. *Social Policy and Administration* 27(1): 50–58.

MacPherson, S. (1993) Social Assistance in Hong Kong. In *Asia Regional Conference on Social Security September 14–16, 1993*, Hong Kong Council of Social Services. Hong Kong: Hong Kong Council of Social Services, 387–412.

MacPherson, S. and J. Midgley (1987) *Comparative social policy and the Third World.* New York: St. Martin's Press.

McLaughlin, E. (1993) Hong Kong: A residual welfare regime. In *Comparing welfare states: Britain in international context*, eds. A. Cochrane and J. Clarke London: Sage, pp. 105–40.

Midgley, J. (1982) *Social security, inequality and the Third World.* Chichester, England: Wiley.

Midgley, J. (1984) *Social Security, inequality and the Third World.* New York: Wiley.

Midgley, J. (1986) Welfare and industrialization: The case of the four little tigers. *Social Policy and Administration* 20(3): 225–238

Midgley, J. (1991) The Radical Right, politics and society. In *The Radical Right and the welfare state: An international assessment*, eds. H. Glennerster and J. Midgley London: Harvester Wheatsheaf, 3–23.

Miners, N. (1993) *The government and politics of Hong Kong.* Hong Kong: Oxford University Press.

Mok, H.T.K. (1993) *Poverty in Hong Kong and social security.* Hong Kong: Chung Wah Books.

Mok, H.T.K. (1994) Elderly in need of care and financial support. In *The other Hong Kong report 1994*, eds. D. McMillen and S. Man. Hong Kong: The Chinese University Press, 315–30.

Scott, I. (1989) *Political change and the crisis of legitimacy in Hong Kong.* Hong Kong: Hurst.

Social Security Society (1991) *Commentary on social security in Hong Kong.* Hong Kong: Social Security Society.

Tang, K.-L. (1996) Social security and social development: East Asian newly industrializing countries (NICs). *Canadian Review of Social Policy* (38): 1–16.

Tsang, S. K. (1991) A contributory social security scheme for Hong Kong: An economic perspective. In *Commentary on Social Security in Hong Kong*, Social Security Society. Hong Kong: Social Security Society, 3–12.

Tsang, S. K. (1994) The economy. In *The other Hong Kong report, 1994*, eds. D. McMillen and S. Man. Hong Kong: The Chinese University Press, 125–48.

Wesley-Smith, P. and A.H.Y. Chen, eds. (1988) *The basic law and Hong Kong's future.* Singapore: Butterworth.

Williamson, J. B. and F.C. Pampel (1993) *Old-age security in comparative perspective.* New York: Oxford University Press.

5

Privatizing Social Security: Relevance of the Chilean Experience

Silvia Borzutzky

The privatization of social security in Chile has been described as a path-breaking solution to the current problems of social security not only in Latin America but throughout the Western world. Undoubtedly the changes that took place in Chile have been profound. They redefined both the functions of the state and the private sector, strengthened capital markets, and created a new set of financial arrangements that transferred the administration of the social security system to the private sector.

In this chapter I analyze the changes introduced by the government of General Pinochet in Chile and discuss its applicability to Western Europe and the United States. Central to this analysis is the belief that Chile's sweeping social security reforms were the product of an authoritarian regime that had suppressed freedom of expression and dissent and had total control of both the executive and the legislative branches of government. Clearly, this centralized and autocratic approach to social security policy making is unworkable in other more democratic societies. Nevertheless, as questions are being asked about the viability of social security in the industrial nations, the Chilean experience has lessons for those who believe that privatization offers an alternative to conventional, insurance-based approaches.

THE PRIVATIZATION OF THE CHILEAN SOCIAL
SECURITY SYSTEM

The reform of social security in Chile is both the result as well as an intrinsic part of the economic and political system imposed upon Chilean society by the regime of General Augusto Pinochet. From the very beginning, the Pinochet regime pursued the destruction of Chile's democratic institutions, the depolitization of the society, and the creation of an authoritarian state. Arguing that the interventionist state of the past was responsible for the country's economic problems, the regime declared that "the state should only assume responsibility for those functions which intermediate or lower level social groups are unable to deal with" (Chile, 1974: 29). Accordingly, it was believed that state involvement in the economy and in the provision of social services impaired the full development of the society. This idea was, of course, inspired by the neoliberal market ideology of Milton Friedman and Frederick von Hayek. Their views were applied in Chile by a group of economists known as the Chicago Boys.

From a political point of view, the regime found legitimacy in the 1980 constitution, which established an authoritarian system, consolidated power in the hands of General Pinochet, and established a system of personal rule that would last at least until 1989. At the same time, the constitution institutionalized a reduction in the functions of the state by transferring many of these functions to the private sector. It also atomized society by limiting channels of political participation and enhancing the role of the market as the regulator of socioeconomic activity (Borzutzky, 1982) The neoliberal economic model then became part of the constitutional makeup of the country. The constitution established a symbiotic relationship between the authoritarian regime and market-oriented policies. As General Pinochet and his advisors argued repeatedly; "The economic strategy and the political system are indivisible parts of the social fabric and both of them have provided the inspiration for the new institutionality" (De Castro, 1981).

Karl Polanyi argued in *The Great Transformation* that in Great Britain "the road to the free market was opened and kept open by an enormous increase in continuous, centrally organized and controlled interventionism" and "that laissez-faire was not a method to achieve a thing, it was the thing to be achieved" (Polanyi, 1944: 139). In Chile, as well as in Great Britain, the establishment of a market system required the transformation of the existing societal structures through state action. In Chile the laws that carried out those changes were known as the "modernizations." The modernizations aimed at restructuring labor, land, and capital markets as well as transforming the education, health, and social security systems. These laws set the basis for a silent revolution, which changed the nature and role of the state, set new parameters for the relations between the public and private sectors, destroyed organized opposition, and established the basis for a new belief system. Through its policies, the regime totally transformed the structure of rural property, the principles that guided the educational system, the organization and power of municipalities, the labor laws that regulated the unions and the professional associations, and the social security system. The health system was only partially modified. Minister of Labor José Piñera led the process of social security and labor reform.

The History of Social Security Privatization in Chile

The privatization of Chile's social security system took place in three stages. First, on October 1, 1973, only nineteen days after the *coup d'etat* that brought General Pinochet to power, the government unified by decree the country's various family allowance funds, replacing them with one *Sistema Unico de Prestaciones Familiares*. Further modifications took place in 1978, when the administration of the family allowances program was taken away from the pension funds and given to newly created entities known as the *Cajas de Compensación de la Asignación Familiar* (Borzutzky, 1982).

The enactment of Decree 2448 in February of 1979 was the second step in the transformation of social security. Without any warning or discussion of any sort, the government enacted this decree, which equalized benefits, eliminated pensions based on years of service, and established a uniform system of pension adjustments. The new decree set the minimum retirement age at sixty-five years for males and sixty for females. It also required at least ten years of contributions to qualify for a pension. Furthermore, the decree eliminated all existing pensions based on years of service, repealed all the existing legislation regarding the re-adjustment of pensions, and established a general, uniform system of re-adjustability that tied pensions to the consumer price index. With a stroke of the pen, the administration eliminated the *perseguidoras*, which were a special type of pension received by the upper echelons of the civil service in which the value of the pension was tied to the value of the salary received by the employee. Decree 2448 had great financial and political significance. There is no doubt that the decree addressed the two most critical problems of the social security system, namely the inequity and insufficiency of pensions. It also eliminated its most costly elements: pensions based on years of service and the *perseguidoras*.

From a historical perspective, the reforms instituted by Decree 2448 and the earlier 1973 decree affecting the family allowance system demonstrate a large degree of continuity with the reforms previously proposed by the Frei administration. But what President Frei could not achieve in a democratic context the authoritarian regime accomplished easily. The group most affected by the reform, the civil servants, who in the past were powerful enough to prevent any substantial reform of their system, were unable to do anything on this occasion. The civil servants learned, just as others had already learned, that an authoritarian government operates with a large degree of autonomy even from the most organized and previously powerful social groups.

The third step in the process of privatizing social security in Chile was completed with the enactment of Decree 3500, which became law in November of 1980 and began to operate in 1981. This decree created a new pension system for workers in both the private and the public sectors. Only the military was exempted. Workers were permitted to join the new pension system on a voluntary basis but incentives were offered to those who joined. The deterioration of the existing state-managed system also facilitated the transfer of many workers to the new system (Borzutzky, 1982). The decree had a major impact. According to its authors, it placed "Chile at the forefront of social security reform in Latin America" (Kast, 1981: 1).

Financial and Administrative Changes

The transformation of the social security system involved both financial and administrative changes. Both will be discussed and reference will also be made to their political and economic impacts.

From a financial standpoint, the 1980 reform effectively eliminated the employer's contributions to the social security system, and the transformation of the previous collective funding system that pooled risks into individual, capitalized funds. The 1980 legislation retained only a 1 percent contribution to the workmen's compensation fund, and a temporary 2.85 percent tax to finance the family allowance and unemployment insurance programs.

Before employers' contributions were abolished in 1981, the government had previously begun to reduce their contribution. This process began in 1975 when contributions were gradually reduced over a five year period from 43.3 percent of taxable wages to 20.3 percent. The purpose of these reductions was to lower the cost of labor and in turn reduce unemployment. Employee contributions were also reduced for those workers who transferred to the new social security system. As was noted earlier, this provided a very strong incentive for workers to transfer. Currently, the employer pays only 0.85 percent to the workmen's compensation fund and 2 percent into the unemployment fund.

These large reductions in contributions to the pension plan were achieved through reductions in social security expenditures due to the elimination of pensions based on years of service, the increase in the retirement age to sixty years for women and sixty-five for men, and the elimination of the *desahucio*, or lump-sum cash benefit based on years of service paid upon retirement.

The common fund, *sistema de reparto*, which had been under attack by neoliberals since 1974, was replaced by individual capitalization funds. For Minister Píñera, the common fund had not only failed to achieve its fundamental purpose—social solidarity—but had generated and encouraged inequalities, inefficiencies, and insufficiencies that characterized the whole social security system. Logically, then, the problem had to be attacked at its roots, by replacing a system based on the collectivist ideology with one based on an ideology that "establishes a clear relationship between the personal effort and the reward," the one "that gives the individual the freedom of choosing and deciding" (Píñera, 1980: 2). The elimination of the common fund, in fact, complemented the elimination of the social security tax and established a compulsory savings system managed by private enterprise. In the new system, workers make regular income-related contributions into individualized savings accounts, which are invested to generate sufficient income to provide retirement, invalidity, and survivor's pensions.

In terms of administrative changes, the transfer of responsibility to private providers was the most significant. The principle of subsidiarity of the state, the need to enhance the role of the private sector, and the improvement of administration led Piñera to argue that social security should be put in the hands of the private sector. Moreover, according to Piñera, privitization would not only benefit future pensioners, but integrate the social security system into the national economy.

It is important to note that for government economists one of the major obstacles to Chile's economic development, and one that the market approach had proven unable to resolve, was the low savings rate that resulted from the underdevelopment of local capital markets. In this context, social security reform was highly beneficial for the development of the capital markets and this for the promotion of economic growth. As Martin Cóstabal argued:

The growth of the capital markets produced by the new pension system will be oriented to producing long-term effects. The long-term characteristics of the social security savings will be geared to develop long-term credit instruments, which would contribute to structuring an integral capital market, something we have not had until now. The development of these long-term capital markets would bring stability and longer terms to the credit system, improving credit conditions for such activities as housing, and for medium and small entrepreneurs, who are intensive credit users. (1981:4[author's translation])

The transference of the administration of social security to the private sector involved the creation of a new enterprises known as the *Administra-*

doras de Fondos de Pensiones or AFPs as they are also known. These pension fund management corporations are responsible for the administration of the individual funds and the provision of social security benefits as established by law. In order to understand the nature and functions of these entities, one has to keep in mind that Decree 3500 contains both free-market and regulatory principles. The free-market principles encourage the formation of a plurality of pension management funds that would compete among themselves, offering different rates of interest on the capital invested in the individual accounts, and charging the lowest commissions. The funds have since proven to be highly lucrative enterprises, whose profits result from the commissions they charge individuals for managing their savings. Commissions are charged in different ways, either as a flat rate, as a percentage of the insured deposit, or as a combination of both. In order to insure efficiency and the lowest commissions, individuals are free to move their savings from one management fund to another.

Given the underdevelopment of the Chilean economy, and especially the underdevelopment of the country's capital markets, the state chose to regulate the investments of the newly created corporations. The law establishes that each management fund has to maintain two separate funds: a minimum capital guarantee fund required to establish an AFP, and a second one formed by the individual deposits. The law also prescribes investment policies and the profitability of the investment fund (Illanes, 1981).

With regard to benefits, the 1980 legislation and the modifications to the law approved in 1987 established that once employees meet the basic requirements for a pension, they have three options. First, they may use their accumulated funds to purchase an immediate life annuity from an insurance company. Second, they may obtain a pension directly from the AFP with which they had saved. However, in this case the capital fund has to be large enough to provide for a pension that is at least equal to 120 percent of the value of the minimum state pension. Third, they may combine a temporary annuity paid by the AFP with a deferred life annuity bought from an insurance company.

Finally, Decree 3500 created a system of minimum pensions to be applied in case of depletion of the individual capital account, or if the income produced by the fund is smaller than the minimum state pension. In order to qualify for this pension, the insured must have at least twenty years of contributions. The original value of the pension was about U.S. $45 monthly.

In addition to fostering the creation of a plethora of pension management funds, the state also created two new agencies, the *Superintendencia,* which supervises the different funds, and the *Instituto de Normalización Previsiónal,* or Institute for the Normalization of the Social Security System, which is charged with coordinating the transition from the old to the new system.

The New System in Operation

Launching the new system involved both the private and the public sectors. The private sector responded by creating new funds, while the state made affiliation to the new system compulsory for all those who became employed for the first time after December of 1982 to ensure that transfers to the new system were permanent.

The beginning of the new system was preceded by the creation of several AFPs. However, the large degree of concentration of the Chilean economy thwarted the free-market principles that inspired the reform. Of the twelve management funds that were established, nine were owned by Chile's largest economic groups and they covered 91.99 percent of the affiliates that changed to the new system. Furthermore, the two largest funds, the *Provida* and *Santa María*, captured 63 percent of the new members in the system. By the end of 1993, *Provida* had about 30 percent of the affiliates, while *Santa María* had 20 percent.

The launching of the reform in 1981 was followed by the massive adoption of the new system. In the first month, half a million people changed to the new system and by December of 1981 more than 1,604,000 persons out of an economically active population of 2,890,000 had moved to the new system. Neither the government nor the funds had predicted such a large move. Currently, 2,808,611 persons are enrolled in the new system. Four elements seem to have prompted people to abandon the old social security system. First, people were encouraged to join through a very expensive and well-orchestrated propaganda campaign. Second, those who moved to the new system were assured a net increase in income through reduced contributions. Third, the old social insurance system was in serious decline, and many workers feared that they would lose their pension rights if they did not transfer to the new system. Finally, many employers pressured their workers to join the new system.

Although both the AFPs and the government launched what was undoubtedly the most expensive publicity campaign in Chile's history, the acceptance of the new system cannot be explained only in terms of skillful propaganda. Probably the most important factor was the net salary increase obtained by those workers who moved the new system. The salary increase ranged from 7.6 percent, for those who belonged to the blue-collar insurance fund to 17.1 percent for members of the bank employees fund. However, since then perceptions of the efficiency of the funds have changed. A survey conducted in 1987 indicates that the public image of these institutions is not favorable. More than 59 percent of the respondents indicated that they believed the state was more likely to pay a higher pension and an indexed pension than the funds, while only 9 percent preferred to leave the administration of the pension programs to national private enterprises. Moreover, the full impact of the salary increases remains to be seen for it depends on the nature and structure of the commissions charged by the AFPs (Baeza, 1986).

The Role of the State

The social security reform does not eliminate the role of the state as neoliberal rhetoric might suggest, but simply transforms it. Two characteristics of this new role are noteworthy: the compulsory nature of the new system, for all new workers are obliged to join the new system, and the creation of two new bureaucracies to supervise the system. As noted earlier, the new system involved the creation of two new social security bureaucracies: the *Superintendencia de Administradoras de Fondos de Pensiones* and the *Instituto de Normalización Previsiónal.* The old *Superintendencia de Seguridad Social* was retained to control the old system. The establishment of a state-enforced private insurance system is certainly unique and reflects a contradiction in neoliberal ideology, namely, the combination of statism with *laissez-faire* capitalism. In order to understand the extent of this contradiction, it must be remembered that the government has consistently asserted that the new system is designed to enhance the freedoms of the Chilean workers. The compulsory aspects of the system reflect both the authoritarian nature of the regime and a paternalistic approach to policy making (Borzutzky, 1982).

Why did a government that had done its utmost to reduce the size of the civil bureaucracy create a large, new supervisory agency in the social security field? Behind the stated technical reasons seems to be a political motive: to create an institution responsive to the needs and ideas of neoliberal economists, and to end the power of the old *superintendencia.* The creation of the new institute is the culmination of a process of fiscal centralization that had begun in 1978 and that drastically reduced the power and functions of the old funds.

THE IMPACT OF PRIVATIZATION

As Minister Píñera argued, the privatization of social security in Chile has been one of the Pinochet regime's most important policy decisions. It constitutes a new and original scheme that will contribute decisively to changing the economic, social, and political culture of all Chileans (Píñera, 1980: 12). As such, it constituted one of the regime's most important modernizations. Of these modernizations, social security reform was significant to Chile's economy and its politics, and it affected the future of the entire population. The impact of this reform can be analyzed in two ways: from an economic perspective and second from a sociopolitical perspective.

Pensions received by insured persons under the new system are directly based on the deposits made by individuals. The total pension is based on deposits plus the interest accrued, less the commissions charged by the AFPs. The deposits, in turn, depend on the level of wages, while the interest depends on the real rate of capital return. With regard to wages, it is important to note that because of the nature of the economic policies pursued by the Pinochet regime, the real value of wages grew at a rate of only 1.2 percent between 1980 and 1988, while the real minimum wage declined by 28.5 percent. During the same period, urban unemployment averaged 15.3 percent per year. Clearly, both indicators have a negative impact on the value of the pensions. Despite these indicators, the government estimated in 1987 that the value of a retirement pension paid by the new system was 1.24 times higher than one paid by the old system, while invalidity pensions appeared to be 2.23 times higher.

The commissions charged by the AFPs also affect the value of the pensions. As it stands now, after several reforms, the funds usually charge two commissions: a fixed sum deducted from the old-age contribution and a variable percentage deducted from the contribution to the disability and survivor's fund. Until 1987, there was a third commission consisting of a percentage over the balance in the individual account. The fixed commission has a regressive effect on the pensions. Mesa-Lago estimated that in 1987 the commission reduced the deposits of a person in the 10,000 pesos per month bracket by 18 percent, while it reduced the fund by 0.99 percent in case of an insured in the 100,000 pesos bracket. Mesa-Lago argued also that for the same reason between 1981 and 1987 the investment yield for the lowest income bracket averaged 7.6 percent, compared with 11.34 percent for the 60,000 peso bracket (Mesa-Lago, 1994). Recent changes in the structure of the commissions have reduced their cost. The total combined commission declined from 3.6 percent in 1983 to 3.1 in 1991. While the cost for someone with an average salary increased from 8.3 percent in 1981 to 12.3 percent in 1983, it declined to 9 percent in 1991 (Mesa-Lago, 1994).

With regard to equity, the system reinforces or augments social and economic inequities. Specifically, the system reinforces the differences between male and female pensions, making female pensions considerably lower because women have a lower retirement age and live longer. It has a regressive effect on the poor due to the existence of the fixed commission. Furthermore, the new system reinforces income differences particularly in the context of the labor laws of the economic policies pursued by the Pinochet regime. These policies had a negative effect on the level of wages and also on the level of pensions. Finally, by excluding the military from the new system, the law protected the existence of a privileged pension fund for the military.

Both the monthly average pension ($75) and the public assistance pension ($36) are insufficient to meet even the most basic needs of people. Moreover, about 37 percent of those who have funds under the AFP system will obtain a pension that is below the minimum pension. In view of this fact, a large proportion of Chile's population will face extreme poverty after retirement (Iglesias and Acuña, 1991).

With regard to the administrative structure of the system, several issues need to be emphasized. First, the capital accumulated by the funds amounts to about $10 billion or 34.5 percent of GDP. It is projected that the funds will reach 50 percent of GDP in the year 2000. The average annual real yield for the 1981–1991 period was 14 percent, the highest for the Latin American region (Mesa-Lago, 1994: 140) Despite the large amounts of capital accumulated by the funds, the capital market has not grown as fast as was expected. By 1991, about one third of the capital of the funds was invested in bonds and shares. The lack of growth of the capital markets was probably due to the numerous regulations on the investments contained in the 1980 law, which was later liberalized.

The ownership of the AFPs was from the beginning tied to dominant economic groups that, as was noted earlier, are the large conglomerates that emerged as a result of the privatization policies of the 1974–1976 period. Originally, the largest funds were owned by the two largest economic groups: the *Vial* and the *Cruzat-Larrain*. Following the recession in 1982, these groups went bankrupt and their assets were temporarily administered by the state. Later, their assets were reprivatized and sold to foreign creditors as part of a "debt for equity scheme" according to which foreign creditors are encouraged to transform their credits in Chile into assets. By 1987, the four largest AFPs were either totally or partially owned by foreign investors. The two largest funds, *Provida* and *Santa María*, are controlled by Bankers Trust and Aetna (Errázuriz, 1987). This development reflects the wider process of denationalization of the entire economy and affects the country's level of savings and investment.

The effects of social security privatiziation on the public sector are just as important as those on the private sector. The privatization of the Chilean social security system has resulted in a budget deficit. This is the result of the costs transfer of the system and with it the payment of contributions to the private sector, as well as the high level of expenditures required to maintain those who remain in the old system. During the first five years, deficits in the state social security system resulted from the fact that the government receipts were drastically reduced due to the massive transfer of people to the new private system. But this reduction in government receipts was not accompanied by a decrease in social security expenditures because in order to allow the AFPs to capitalize, the law stipulated that they would not pay pensions during the first five years. As a result, during the first five years, the state was responsible for meeting the needs of those who retired.

Even after the competition from privitization of the first five years, state expenditures on social security have continued to be sizable because of the *bono de reconocimiento*, or bonus payment, that is paid to those who retire in the new system. This payment, which represents the number of years that the insured contributed to the old system, becomes effective at the time of retirement, invalidity or death. By 1983, the government's social security deficit reached 7 percent of GDP, and a large part of it resulted from the privatization (Arellano, 1989). It is estimated that by the year 2000, the government would have paid no less than 208,400 bonds at an enormous public cost (Garcia, 1986). Another financial burden arises from the fact that many civil servants have been very reluctant to move to the new system. The civil servants fund requires a large state contribution and continues to present a sizable burden on public resources.

A recent study by Iglesias and Acuña (1991) established that the state social security deficit amounted to 1.2 percent of GDP in 1981, 3.2 percent in 1982, and 3.9 percent in 1984. In the subsequent years it has fluctuated around 3.3 percent of GDP. These analysts argue also that about 89 percent of the deficit is the result of operational costs, while only 11 percent is the result of the *bono de reconocimiento*. However, these estimates are fairly low compared with those made by Gillion and Bonilla (1992), who contend that the state subsidy to social security for 1990 amounted to 6percent of GDP. It is not clear how this deficit will be financed. While Iglesias and Acuña (1991) suggest that it has been financed with internal savings, others emphasize the use of taxes, public debt, or reduction in consumption. The deficit is expected to increase at least until the year 2000. As Mesa-Lago (1994) noted, the state made a huge financial commitment to secure a sound private pension system in the long term.

This large deficit and continued government budgetary commitment to the social security system contradict the government's original assertion that the privatization of the social security system would solve the huge fiscal problems created by the old system. This fact leads one to conclude that the decision to privatize the system was primarily an ideological one. Interviews with policy makers in 1981 led the author to conclude that the impact of the reform on the state's fiscal situation was never estimated and that a commitment to subsidiarity rather than fiscal responsibility motivated the change. Consequently, the privatization of social security has had a major budgetary impact, that will seriously affect the finances of the Chilean state in the future.

Another economic impact concerns the administrative costs of the system. From the beginning, the authors of the reform maintained that the new system would reduce costs dramatically (Piñera, 1991). Enrollment in the new system was treated as a commercial product to be sold in the market. Competition, it was believed, would reduce administrative costs considerably. However, enrollment in the APFs depends on their marketing effectiveness. This involves considerable expense and has in fact resulted in an increase in administrative load. About 8,000 people are currently involved in the administration of the funds (about 30 percent of them are sales persons), while there were previously about 7,000 in the administration of the old system (Mesa-Lago, 1994).

It is clear that the administrative costs have not been reduced as a result of privatization. It appears that the new system is more expensive than the old one. In 1980, the administrative cost of the social security system amounted to about 8 percent of contributions; this figure increased to 19 percent in 1982. In 1990, it declined to 14 percent (Iglesias and Acuña, 1991). Also, administrative costs in Chile are higher than those of most of the other Latin American countries. In Argentina, Costa Rica, and Panama, administrative expenses amount to about 7 percent of contributions, while in Uruguay and the Dominican Republic they are about 11 percent (Iglesias and Acuña, 1991).

Social and Political Impact

An important question from a social point of view is to what extent the privatization of social security in Chile has altered traditional social security principles. There is little doubt that the reform has substantially transformed the principle of social solidarity on which the old system was based. Social security in many other countries is also based on this principle. In other words, the contingency of retirement now becomes the responsibility of the individual rather than the community as a whole. The only exception is the case of those who are too poor to meet their own needs. As the undersecretary of labor told the author in an interview, the reform transforms the notion of solidarity both in its role and in its content. From now on, solidarity is not a fundamental value but a complementary notion and as such it is not expressed in the entire social security system, but is reserved for those cases in which the principle of individual responsibility cannot be applied. To a large extent then, privatization has transformed the social security system into a private insurance system in which the state intervenes at two different stages, first, at the onset by enforcing enrollment into the new system, and at the final stage by providing pensions to the lowest income groups.

From a political perspective, the reform has to be analyzed in the context of the other reforms enacted by the government between 1981 and 1982. It is clear that the neoliberal economic model and the authoritarian state converge in their need to disarticulate the entire society, and especially those groups perceived as having political power and interfering with the free functioning of the market. These groups include organized labor and professional associations of white-collar workers and civil servants (Borzutzky, 1982). During the last fifty years, there has been a close relationship between the labor movement and the state, with particular reference to the social security system. After having reformed the role and functions of the state, and the nature of the labor movement, the Pinochet regime created a new social security system more attuned to those reforms. Of course, in an authoritarian context, the reforms came from the state itself, without the participation of the society. Social security reform destroyed large bureaucratic entities, such as the pension funds, as well as the groups of workers organized around them, who in the past had played a major role both in the formulation and in the obstruction of public policies. Clearly, social security reform in Chile has been a key political mechanism for shaping future political arrangements.

RELEVANCE TO THE INDUSTRIAL NATIONS

Although the evolution of social security in Western European countries was quite different from that in the United States, in both places the system evolved in response to societal pressures arising from processes of economic change and the actions of governments responsive to those pressures. Many writers have shown that social security is fundamentally associated with politics and the reaction of the state to the influence of organized groups. In Latin America, either under democratic or populist regimes, similar processes operated. Different pressure groups, political parties, and the state interacted to produce large but fragmented and unequal social security systems.

The privatization of social security in Chile is a significant deviation from this trend. An authoritarian state was the initiator of a radical transformation of an existing social security system. The privatization of social security in Chile not only took place under an extremely authoritarian and centralized regime, but it was also an intrinsic part of a process by which the regime entirely changed the social and economic role of the state and the nature of state-society relations. Both the regime and the policy-making process were undemocratic, and those affected by policy decisions were excluded from participating in the process. The Chilean system seems to be incompatible with current views about social policy in Europe and the United States.

This is true also of the few Latin American countries that have been inspired by the Chilean experiment. In Latin America, the Chilean model has been emulated by Peru, Argentina, and Colombia. Between 1993 and 1994, these countries privatized their pension funds to some degree. These countries have political systems that are either totally authoritarian, as in Peru, or partially democratic as in Argentina. However, the adoption of these new systems has been fairly slow. In Argentina, after spending millions of dollars to promote private funds, only 50,000 persons enrolled.

However, the question of the reduction of the functions of the state and privatization of social security has become an issue in the United States, Great Britain, and some European countries. A reduction in the role of the state in these countries is seen as one answer to the economic problems of the late 1970s and 1980s. As Scarpaci argued, "Its great popular appeal is that it proposes to curtail public spending, increase cash reserves, and reduce taxes" (Scarpaci, 1988: 1).

In Europe, reductions in social programs have been closely associated with economic difficulties. However, only Great Britain has introduced significant changes, seeking, for example, to introduce internal markets in the national health care system and fostering the growth of private pension funds. For the most part, other European governments have introduced marginal reforms geared to reducing specific benefits, rather than privatizing the system.

In the United States, discussion on the future viability of social security has increased, but no significant changes have yet been introduced. Given the entrenched pluralism of the American system, significant changes in social security are unlikely. It is partly that the political system in the United States does not lend itself to radical change, but it is also a consequence of the fact that American social security has remained separated from other welfare programs, particularly social assistance. "In the United States, various social benefits remain operationally, fiscally, and symbolically separate from one another, and they are all kept quite apart from other things the national government may be doing in relation to the economy and society" (Weir, Orloff, and Skocpol, 1988: 9). This unique characteristic of the U.S. system impedes significant change. Another factor is that since the 1950s, social security has been politically protected by a strong bureaucracy and a broad base of public support. Over the years, political support for the program has increased at a pace with the increase in benefits. Given the nature of the political system, calls for sweeping policy changes translate into budget cuts that would affect the poor, while universal benefits and programs for the middle class would be left intact.

In examining the applicability of the Chilean model to Western Europe and the United States, it is important to stress the uniqueness of the Chilean experience. The privatization of social security in Chilean was the result of very unique political and economic arrangements that existed in Chile in 1980. It is unlikely that similar policy proposals will be adopted in Europe and the United States. The transformation of social security in Chile was the result of a break with the past that is only possible in the context of revolutionary or counterrevolutionary situations. However, the reform has not fulfilled its promise. As has been shown already, its economic, administrative, and social impact has not been beneficial, despite claims to the contrary. The fact that it is unlikely to be adopted in the advanced welfare states is, therefore, to be welcomed. Indeed, it is to be hoped that the negative lessons of the Chilean privatization will serve as a warning to those who believe that the privatization of collective provision will enhance the well-being of the people.

REFERENCES

Arellano, J. P. (1989) La Seguridad Social en Chile en los años 90. *Coleccion estudios cieplan* 27: 63–83.

Arellano, J. P. (1986) Una Mirada Critica a la Reforma de 1981. *Anàlisis de la previsión en Chile*, ed. S. Baeza. Santaigo: Centro de Estudios Públicos, 81–93.

Baeza, S., ed. (1986) *Anàlisis de la previsión en Chile.* Santiago: Centro de Estudios P:aaublicos.

Borzutzky, S. (1982) *Chilean politics and social security policies* Ph.D. Dissertation, University of Pittsburgh.

Borzutzky, S. (1986) Políticas y reformas de la seguridad social. In *La crísis de la seguridad social y la atención a la Salud*, ed. C. Mesa-Lago. México: Fondo de Cultura Económica, 285–303.

Borzutzky, S. (1991) The Chicago boys, social security and welfare in Chile. In *The Radical Right and the welfare state*, eds. H. Glennerster and J. Midgley. London: Harvester Wheatsheaf, 79–99.

Borzutzky, S. (1993) Social security and health policies in Latin America: The changing roles of the state and the private sector. *Latin American Research Review* 28(3): 246–56.

Chile, Government (1974) *Declaration of principles.* Santiago: Gobierno de Chile.

Cóstabal, M. (1981) Efectos económicos de la reforma previsional. *Gestión* 6(64): 1–10.

De Castro, S. (1981) *El estado de las finanzas públicas.* Speech published in *El Mecurio*, 15 January, 1981, p. 1.

Errázuriz, E. (1987) *Capitalización de la deuda externa y desnacionalización de la economía.* Santiagao: Program de Economia del Trabajo, no. 57.

García, J. A. (1986) Mercado de renta vitalicia y bono de reconocimiento. In *Anàlisis de la previsión en Chile*, ed. S. Baeza. Santiago: Centro de Estudios Públicos, 165–192.

Gillion, C. and A. Bonilla (1992) Analysis of a national pension scheme: The case of Chile. *International Labour Review* 131(2): 171–95.

Iglesias, A. and R. Acuña (1991) *Experiencia con un regimen de capitalización, 1981–1991.* Santiago: Cepal/Pnud.

Illanes, E. (1981) Inversión de recursos del sistema de pensiones. *Gestión* 6(63): 48–52.

Kast, M. (1981) *La Nación*, 20 June.

Mesa-Lago, C. (1989) *Ascent to bankruptcy: Financing social security in latin america.* Pittsburgh: University of Pittsburgh Press.

Mesa-Lago, C. (1991) *Social security and economic adjustment restructuring in Latin*

America and the Caribbean: A study for the international labour office. Pittburgh, PA: University of Pittbrugh, Department of Political Science, unpublished manscript.

Mesa-Lago, C. (1994) *Changing social security in Latin America and the Caribbean: Towards the alleviation of social costs of economic reform.* Boulder, Colorado: Lynne Reiner.

Montecinos, V. (1993) *Economic reforms and women in Chile.* Unpublished manuscript.

Piñera, J. (1980) *Seminario sobre reforma previsional y plan laboral.* Speech delivered on 29 June 1980. Santiago: Ministry of Labor.

Piñera, J. (1991) *El casabel al gato: La batalla por la reforma previsional.* Santiago: Zig-Zag.

Polanyi, K. (1944) *The great transformation.* Boston: Beacon Press.

Scarpaci, J., ed. (1988) *Health services privatization in industrial societies.* Pittsburgh: University of Pittsburgh Press.

Weir, M., Orloff, S., and T. Skocpol (1988) *The politics of social policy in the United States.* New Jersey: Princeton University Press.

6

Pension Reform in Britain: Alternative Modes of Provision

Matthew Owen and Frank Field

Of the many challenges facing social security programs in the industrial countries today, the stress placed on social security resources by an aging population is perhaps the most serious. Providing an adequate and affordable level of retirement pension is no longer as straightforward as the founders of social security originally believed it would be. While state social security systems in the industrial countries provided reasonably adequate protection to the elderly in the decades following World War II, their ability to continue to do so in the future is becoming increasingly strained as more people survive into old age and as the proportion of the population in gainful employment declines.

The fact that social security programs are funded on a pay-as-you-go basis means that the social security taxes paid by those in employment are directly transferred to meet the needs of those in retirement. As needs have increased and social security costs have risen, serious fiscal pressures have been created. The notion that social security contributions are a form of insurance designed to guarantee payments in the future is being undermined. Today more younger people doubt that social security will provide for their own needs when they themselves retire.

The failure of the governments of the Western industrial countries to address this problem in meaningful ways has exacerbated the concerns of many younger people about the future of social security. As popular news reports have sensationalized the problem, there is a danger that the very foundations on which social security rests may be subverted by a crisis of legitimacy. If people doubt that the social security system will remain solvent and meet their own retirement needs, they will be reluctant to contribute and pressure for its abolition will increase. It is in this climate that various proposals for the reform of social security need to be considered.

Some have proposed that social security should be replaced with Chilean-style individualized compulsory savings accounts funded exclusively by the contributions of members. Others have suggested that any form of state managed and operated social security should be abandoned and that the private insurance and occupational pension markets should assume responsibility for meeting people's needs in retirement. Others have contended that a private system of pensions should comprise a primary form of social protection in retirement but that a safety net social assistance scheme operated by the government should function to help those who are unable to secure protection through private sources. Yet others have argued that relatively simple modifications to conventional social security systems can be introduced to insure their solvency and ability to meet the needs of an aging population in the future. In some countries, such as the United States, steps have already been taken to secure the solvency of the social system by reducing expenditures and increasing revenues through higher contributions.

This chapter examines the situation in Britain and offers a relatively simple and realistic set of proposals for addressing the challenge of providing adequate social security protection for old-age retirement. The proposals outlined in this chapter were originally published in *The Fabian Review*(Fields and Owen, 1993). We recommend that the existing state social security system be augmented by the requirement that every employed and self-employed person obtain additional social protection through a private occupational pension fund. The current system of insuring basic social protection for all through the statutory social insurance system will continue but will be augmented by mandatory, universal private protection. In this regard, it simply extends the current two-tier system of state and private provision enjoyed by millions of British workers to the whole population. Before outlining these proposals in more detail, the current system and its historical evolution will be described.

SOCIAL SECURITY IN BRITAIN

Social security in Britain today consists of various income maintenance programs based on different approaches to funding. Unlike the United States, where the term social security is used to refer exclusively to the federal government's old-age retirement, survivors, and disability insurance program, in Britain the term has a broader connotation, referring not only to insurance-funded programs but to means-tested social assistance and universal social allowances as well.

Social insurance is the preferred approach to social security. It currently covers contingencies such as old-age retirement, death, unemployment, and employment injury. The scheme is managed by the central government. Maternity and sickness benefits were previously provided through social insurance as well, but they are today incorporated into a employer liability system by which employers are reimbursed by the social insurance fund for payments made to workers who are granted sickness and maternity leave.

Social assistance in Britain caters to people with various needs who have low incomes. Eligibility for assistance is determined by an income test that is known as the means test. A range of benefits are available through the central government's social assistance program and in addition the municipalities provide various social assistance benefits as well.

The central government also manages a social allowance system that pays benefits to families with children and the disabled without regard to income. Funded from general tax revenues, it may be viewed as a subsidy paid by the state to those who have additional income needs. The child benefit program is very popular with parents even though the amount paid is quite small. Nevertheless, this amount is widely viewed as a helpful way of defraying the additional costs associated with child rearing.

In addition to these three statutory modes of social security provision, British citizens have access to a plethora of private occupational pensions and commercial savings and insurance schemes that also function to provide social protection. These provisions are often supported by tax concessions and comprise a part of what Titmuss (1958) described as the fiscal welfare system. Although proponents of state welfare have often regarded these provisions with disdain, believing that they will someday be replaced with statutory programs, they have continued to play an important role and comprise what Evans and Piachaud (1996) described as a fourth "pillar" of British social security. As will be argued, the private pillar can be integrated with the statutory system to comprise a comprehensive and effective system of social security that offers adequate social protection to the elderly during retirement.

The Evolution of the British Social Security System

As with so much of Britain's social security system, current pension provision still bears traces of its nineteenth-century origins. National allowances for the elderly were first proposed in the 1890s in light of the insurance-funded programs that were introduced in Germany in the previous decade by Chancellor Otto von Bismarck (Fraser, 1973), the overriding principle in these proposals was that of insurance. That is to say, provision was seen in terms of insuring individuals against the contingency of their growing old and being unable to earn a living. When life expectancies correlated with people's working life, insurance was a perfectly rational mode of provision. During the early years of this century, when working men's compensation against industrial injury and unemployment was being advocated by the Liberal party, insurance against aging was a natural addition to the platform for full national insurance.

Initially however, Britain did not introduce an insurance-funded old-age retirement system. Instead, the 1908 Old Age Pensions Act adopted the social assistance approach to pay means-tested retirement pensions to needy elderly people over the age of seventy years. The pension was introduced in the wake of bitter debates about the future of the poor laws. Although the pension, like poor relief, was means tested, it was effectively distinguished from the poor laws. Avoiding the stigma associated with application for poor relief, take-up was surprisingly high.

Nevertheless, the insurance approach continued to be favored by reform-minded liberals and socialists alike, who argued that insurance-funded retirement pensions would be "earned" through lifetime contributions and that this would abolish all vestiges of stigma. Nor would pensioners be dependent on the benevolence of the government or subject to the vagaries of budgetary constraints. The insurance approach required that benefits be based on contributions and that they be paid to recipients as of right.

The campaign for social insurance is often seen to have reached its logical conclusion in 1942 with the publication of the Beveridge Report. Nevertheless, the Beveridge Report contained modest proposals. It favored universal flat-rate benefits, and it made clear that these benefits should be paid at a very low level. This was for two reasons. First, higher benefits would require contributions that would be beyond the reach of lower-paid workers and would, therefore, undermine the insurance equation of a fair premium for a fair level of coverage. Second, Beveridge insisted that low benefits were a necessary stimulus to additional private provision. A member of the Liberal party, Beveridge believed that state provision should offer only a basic safety net, while the private sector should provide more extensive protection. Well-established insurance companies, like the Prudential and the Friendly Societies, would, he asserted, have an important role to play. This is perhaps one of the most neglected of Beveridge's proposals, even though it has also been the most effective. By supporting the maintenance of the private sector, Beveridge ensured that Britain today has an extensive and effective private system of care that meets the retirement needs of many millions of people.

Beveridge's proposals were implemented with the enactment of the 1946 National Insurance Act, which established a universal, flat-rate pension for all workers. The act also introduced survivor's, sickness, maternity, death, and unemployment benefits. Despite Beveridge's optimistic belief that the private sector would cater to the needs of most elderly people, a sizable proportion of the working population were wholly dependent on state provision. As may be expected, these were primarily low-income workers and those who changed jobs frequently. At the same time, the private sector responded to the needs of millions of white-collar workers, particularly in the corporate sector, insuring that they had adequate retirement protection.

However, as it became clear that the flat-rate pension was too small to provide sufficient income in retirement for those without private pensions, the Labour party began to campaign for the introduction of income-related pensions. The party proposed that the flat-rate system be replaced with a universal graduated pension. This proposal was rejected by the Conservative government, which in 1959 modified the original Beveridge scheme to permit the awarding of earnings-related pensions for a limited number of pensioners who had no private occupational pensions. This pension was funded by the introduction of earnings-related contributions by all workers.

This change was not, however, regarded as adequate by social security experts within the Labour party, who continued to press for the introduction of universal earnings-related pensions for all. Known as national superannuation, these pensions, some hoped, would eventually replace the private system completely. However, during its 1964–1970 term of office, the Labour party failed to introduce national superannuation and it was only in 1975, when it returned to office, that a more modest graduated scheme known as the State Earnings-Related Pensions Scheme (SERPS) was established. However, this scheme did not seek to abolish private pensions. Instead, it strengthened the private system by permitting workers with approved occupational pensions to "contract-out" of SERPS. This development effectively created a two-tier system of pension provision. Under the new system, all workers would contribute and receive a basic, first-tier state pension. At the second tier, some would have private occupational pensions, while the remainder would be covered by SERPS.

The election of the Thatcher government in 1979 effectively ended the postwar period of welfare state consensus in Britain. Since Mrs. Thatcher's administration was openly committed to replacing state programs with private provisions, it is not surprising that efforts were made to abolish the state earnings-related pension. However, because the private pension industry was unwilling to assume responsibility for the low-paid, high-risk workers catered to by SERPS, the scheme was retained. Nevertheless, the scheme was made less generous and incentives were offered to members of the scheme to seek private coverage through what were known as "personal pension plans" managed by a commercial insurance or investment company. Since 1987, 5 million people have left SERPS to join these plans.

While some have benefitted, others have lost heavily. In 1994, considerable press attention focused on the problems encountered by many of those who left SERPS who had been poorly advised and persuaded to invest their money in unsound schemes through hard-sell advertising techniques. The lessons of this experience must be borne in mind when considering proposals for increasing the involvement of commercial providers in retirement pensions.

The Role of Private Occupational Pensions

Despite the efforts of the proponents of state welfarism, the provision of a basic pension by the state has been only one part of a dual approach to solving the problem of poverty in old age. From the early days, employers have provided occupational pension schemes for their retired employees. For many years, paternalistic employers had rewarded loyal and long-serving members of their work force with discretionary retainers when they retired. However, these payments did not operate within a formal structure and they were open to abuse by employers who could discipline employees by threatening to withhold pensions. Such dependence on the inclinations of employers was consequently an important contributory factor to poverty in old age and the increasing call for state intervention.

The provision by some employers of occupational pensions has a long history. In 1834, the same year as the Poor Law Reform Act was passed, the first formal occupational scheme in Britain was initiated—the Civil Service Occupational Pension Scheme. Very gradually others followed, but it was not until the end of the nineteenth century that schemes were established for white-collar employees in banks, railways, schools, and some utilities. The manufacturing sector followed. A scheme for workers at Lever's factory was, for example, introduced in 1905. In addition, friendly societies attempted to cater to the pension needs of skilled manual workers.

The existence of a mixed economy of pensions did not mean there was systematic coverage. When the basic state pension was created by the 1946 National Insurance Act, less than 10 percent of elderly people received any income from private providers such as occupational pension schemes, friendly societies, and trades unions. This meant that the debate about the level of the state pension was not then influenced, as it is now, by the existence of numerous occupational pension schemes. However, as noted earlier, the introduction of a flat-rate pension under the Beveridge proposals fostered the expansion of the private market. Indeed, less than a decade later the position was changing. By 1953, 6.2 million employees had earned a right to some form of occupational pension, although the coverage was still uneven. Higher-paid workers were more likely than lower-paid workers to be members of an occupational pension scheme, and many more male workers than female workers had acquired these pension rights.

Coinciding with the gradual increase in occupational pension schemes was legislation designed to stimulate such schemes with fiscal incentives. Although tax relief on pension contributions was first introduced by Chamberlain in the 1921 Finance Act, full tax relief on employee and employer contributions was not introduced until 1952 with the Income Tax Act, which significantly boosted occupational schemes. While pension income was taxed, tax relief on contributions meant that pensions were a very attractive savings product.

It was also during this period that personal pensions were introduced. The 1956 Finance Act ensured that the self-employed and those employees not covered by occupational pension schemes could secure individual retirement arrangements with similar tax advantages through insurance companies. These measures became an established, if small, part of pension provision during the 1960s and 1970s, and expanded significantly in the 1980s.

Today the consequence of these fiscal sweeteners is a massive private pensions sector with huge financial assets. In terms of the investments that occupational and personal pension schemes control, over half the British stock market is owed by pension funds. As a result, Britain is one of a handful of nations with significant funded pension liabilities (others include the Netherlands, Canada, and Australia).

THE NEED TO REFORM SOCIAL SECURITY

As noted earlier, one of the greatest challenges facing social security today is the question of how to insure adequate social protection against the contingency of old-age retirement. For much of the postwar period, the response to improving the income of the retired was to increase the value of a state pension paid universally to every person over a certain age. Despite the immense cost of such a strategy, it still commands much respect throughout Europe. Even in Britain where the Conservative government has been in office for a long time, the basic state pension (as the universal minimum pension is known) continues to be the government's single largest budget item.

The future of the basic pension must, however, come under question. In addition to ideological opposition, demographic and fiscal factors place a major burden on public provision. These factors provide ammunition for those on the Right who desire to abolish the state social security provision. As was noted earlier, the Conservative government previously sought to abolish the state earnings-related pension scheme, and it has weakened the basic pension by linking its real value in line with prices rather than wages. This policy decision, which has been in effect since 1983, means that the pension will be worth less than 8 percent of average earnings by the year 2020.

These two policy developments have been instrumental in shaping the debate around social security in Britain. In particular, the lack of a coherent response from opposition parties has meant that the political Right has seized the reforming initiative by championing private provision as the only stable and sustainable option for an aging British population. Indeed, except for the Liberal Democrat party, which has a small number of seats in Parliament, parliamentary opposition has been minimal.

Rather than simply bemoan this situation, or attempt to fight a rearguard action in defense of the status quo, this chapter seeks to outline proposals to reform the current structures of public and private provision that will recognize the sustainability of private modes of provision while at the same time promote a collectivist framework.

These proposals start from the proper recognition of one of the major welfare successes of the postwar period, namely, the spread of occupational and other private sector pension coverage in Britain. It is desirable to build on this success instead of denigrating it as welfare statists have tended to do in the past. It is desirable that this achievement be reinforced by efforts to expand the role of the private sector in providing universal social protection. These arguments are not incompatible with progressive and left-wing beliefs. Indeed, it time for the Left to insist that universal provision is more relevant than ever before, but that universalism should come from the private and not the public sector.

In addition, there are equity considerations that should also appeal to those on the Left. For too long, industry has been able to pass off part of its costs to the taxpayer. Many employers continue to deny pension options to their employees using the existence of the state earnings-related pension as an excuse for evading their responsibility. This effectively means that taxpayers instead of private employers cover the costs of providing old-age protection for many workers. It is time that these costs be returned to the private sector. Employers should be made responsible for the welfare of their employees.

There is an urgent need for a national debate involving government, employers, and employees about how the retirement security of workers can be achieved in the most efficient and equitable way. A debate of this kind is urgent in view of the fact that the problems of an aging society are becoming more serious as the years pass. It is not only that popular press reports and slogans about the future bankruptcy of the social security system are undermining its legitimacy, but that there are real dangers ahead for millions of people who will reach retirement with little, if any, pension entitlement above the basic pension. This threat is made all the more pressing by the rapid growth of long-term unemployment, which denies individuals the right to participate in private pension arrangements.

It is, therefore, imperative that social security policy makers recognize that this decade is perhaps the last time that real reform of pensions can be delivered. This assertion is supported by two observations: First, the transitional costs involved in extending funded provision to a greater number of beneficiaries will never again be cheaper because of the maturing demography of Britain. Second, British politicians will probably never again serve an electorate so poorly informed about long-term savings that major reforms can be implemented without entrenched vested interests blocking reform.

PROVIDING SOCIAL SECURITY THROUGH PRIVATE PROTECTION

At the outset, it is important to emphasize that the proposals outlined here in no way endanger the current state basic pension. These proposals are based on the idea that the government will continue to insure the payment of a state pension to every person over the age of sixty-five through the current pay-as-you-go system. However, the second-tier earnings-related pension would be abolished and replaced with a universal private occupational pension for all.

The proposal for universalizing private coverage is based on the requirement that saving for an additional pension will be compulsory. Although participation in private pensions is currently voluntary, it is fundamentally important that optional participation be ended and that all employers and employees be required to join the scheme. A voluntary scheme will simply not work. Despite the fact that many governments have tried to encourage citizens to save through the use of fiscal incentives, it has proven difficulty to raise savings ratios. Similarly, unless saving for a pension is made compulsory, it is impossible to see how the needs of pensioners will be met in in the next century.

Compulsory participation will extend to all workers, including part-time employees and the self-employed. In addition, those who are currently not protected by the state pension will also be covered. They include the unemployed, the disabled, and those who are out of the labor market because they are caring for someone. Since these persons are unable to contribute to a pension fund, it is proposed that their contributions be paid for them out of government revenues. Contribution rates will be based on average earnings. Of course, if they return to full employment, they will contribute on the same basis as other employees.

Another key element in the proposal concerns funding. It is proposed that the contribution level be set at 10 percent based on rates of 4 percent for employees and 6 percent for employers. Employers will not be able to avoid contributing by hiring part-time workers because contributions will be based on hourly earnings. This requirement is critical in view of the fact that more and more employers are offering jobs without any pension coverage. Related to this requirement will be the creation through legislation of minimum standards that will provide a benchmark against which private pension funds will compete. This notion is further developed later in this chapter where the proposal for a National Pension Savings Scheme is outlined. The national scheme will define these standards and emerge as a pacesetter for the private market.

Another element in the proposal is that workers and the pubic in general be educated about how private pension funds operate. Similarly, their participation in investment and other decisions will be increased. It is very important that employees who are currently ignorant of the workings of the pension industry gain ownership over their pension assets. For this reason, educational programs will be introduced to insure that employees have greater knowledge of the field. At the same time, the industry will be required to be more transparent and accountable. The secretiveness, obscurantism, and jargon of the industry will be replaced by more accessibility. In addition, steps will be taken to enhance regulation of the industry. The government has already enacted legislation that will establish a regulatory agency with wide powers to insure that pension assets are not abused as was the case with the Robert Maxwell scandal. Regulation is the key to the effective use of the private market for pension reform.

Portability of pensions will also be an important consideration. A major drawback of private occupational schemes has been the inability to transfer pension rights when employment changes occur. The reforms introduced in 1975 by the Labour government (which insured inflation proofing of frozen pension assets) and the introduction of actuarially assessed transfer values in 1985 by the Conservative government will be enhanced.

This raises the issue of catering to those who are concerned about preserving pension rights when they transfer employment or who are simply reluctant to invest in private funds. To cater to their needs, it is proposed that a nationwide personal savings plan using the infrastructure of the National Savings be established. As market research has shown, the majority of people perceive pension funds as no different to building society accounts—except that the money cannot be accessed. There is no reason why this perception should be disturbed. Britain's well-established National Saving's tradition of providing long-term, secure savings products can provide an effective mechanism for accumulating pension assets. This institution is one of the best brands in the financial services industry and it is widely respected.

The proposed National Pension Savings Scheme (NPSS) will be voluntary. There will be no requirement that contributions be paid into the NPSS rather than any other private pension scheme. However, as noted earlier, it would provide a minimum standard against which other schemes would compete. Its low administrative charges would make it very attractive to employers and employees alike.

Second, although managed within the framework of the National Savings, it would be independent. This raises the issue of how independent a scheme operated by a body associated with the state can be. One way, suggested by many, would be to have nationally elected trustees to ensure the state cannot dip into the fund. However, this by itself is not enough. Although its structure as a money-purchase scheme would prevent an actuarial surplus from accruing for anyone to plunder, if people's savings are really to be protected, they must be as closely involved with their pension account as they are in any other of their savings. To make the structure totally watertight, the organization could be incorporated through legislation as a mutual society. The National Pension Savings Scheme should, therefore, aim to offer choice in investment strategies in the same way that private funds do. A secure combination of index-tracking funds would be available as a vanilla option but there is no reason why more exotic vehicles should not be available so long as they are understood by consumers.

This leads into the third requirement, namely, the investment of assets. As a fund that is independent of the state, there is no reason why its investment management should not be tendered out to professional fund managers. Likewise, the degree of discretion the manager enjoys should be decided by the scheme members.

Finally, there is the issue of transition costs. How will the reform of the system be financed? Costs will obviously be incurred. There are no easy answers, but there have never been any easy answers whenever society experiences a significant change in its social provisions. Although there will be opposition, it is proposed that these costs be met by removing current tax concessions on the payment of lump sums on pension benefits. The lobby calling for the elimination of a tax-free lump sum and full-tax allowances on all capital gains is growing increasingly vocal. In addition, the abolition of tax relief on pension contributions should also be considered. This would create a level playing field for savings that would extend throughout the financial services industry. In addition to covering transition costs, compulsory pension savings would make tax incentives unnecessary. This last proposal is perhaps the most unpalatable element of the proposals, but it is also the most pressing if the task of mobilizing the needed resources is to be completed.

Concerns and Criticisms

The proposals outlined in this chapter have now gained a certain amount of publicity, and they have support from members of all three major British political parties. Nevertheless, a number of concerns and criticisms of the initial proposals have been made. One of these concerns the assumption that a 10 percent contribution shared between employers and employees will meet the actuarial demands for an adequate pension. This figure is currently being reviewed with reference to the actuarial assumptions used in calculating investment returns.

Another and perhaps more substantial criticism concerns the choice of pension fund. If employees are permitted to choose their own pension schemes, the administrative costs to employers of paying their and their employee's contributions into possibly as many schemes as there are workers would be too great. Furthermore, there has been concern from all political camps that the pensions industry had yet to prove itself a worthy recipient of what, quite literally, will be a deluge of money. While it is still not the case that consumers can have complete faith in the financial industry as a whole, steps will be taken to enhance confidence and participation, as was described earlier.

The issue of regulation aside, it is clear that there are problems of administration costs. Also relevant is the fact that the British are still very immature consumers of financial services of any form. Both factors suggest that there could be some shortcomings in the existing private sector if it suddenly saw demand quadrupling. More specifically, it is necessary for the reforms to be underwritten by a minimum standard scheme with which the private sector can compete. As noted earlier, the proposed NPPS would fulfill this function.

While the use of the private market is proposed here, the nature of the vehicle that individuals have used successfully to accumulate pension savings is in many respects a marginal issue. What matters more is that there is nothing the state can offer that will compete with the security and quality of the provision of the private sector. While it is important to emphasize confidence and security, it is a neglected fact that despite the failings of occupational schemes, their faults pale in significance compared to the unfulfilled promises of state provision. It is, after all, quite fair to say that no form of state pension provision has ever met its original commitments in Britain.

Another concern relates to the issue of compulsory participation. It has been suggested that this requirement is undemocratic and unworkable. Nevertheless, it is absolutely essential that participation be compulsory if the proposed program is to work. Nor is it unjustifiable. The government has, in the past, used its power to require compliance with requirements that are in the best interest of society. In the same way that the state obliges children to attend school and motorists to wear seat belts, there is no sustainable objection to the requirement that everyone make regular contributions to a secondary pension.

A final criticism of these proposals is more ideological than substantive and relates to the traditional dislike of private markets by many on the left of the political spectrum. An example of this is an angry letter denouncing the Fabian Society for publishing the original proposals (Carapiet, 1993). The author maintained that the proposals were "thoroughly Thatcherite" and contrary to the society's socialist traditions. While many on the Left may sympathize with these sentiments, it is unfortunate that the Left has no plausible alternatives to the Conservative government's plans to abolish social security. The proposals outlined here go on the offensive and secure the long-term viability of the basic state pension. While the government is seeking to privatize the universal pension, the proposals offered here stand the government's plan on its head by universalizing the private pension. This approach not only safeguards the social security system but ensures its long viability. In so doing, it also safeguards the interests of millions of pensioners for many decades to come.

REFERENCES

Carapiet, S. (1993) Doing Something Right. *Fabian Review* 105(5): 19.

Evans, M. and D. Piachaud (1996) Social security in Britain: The challenge of needs versus costs. In *Challenges to social security: An international inquiry*, eds. J. Midgley and M. Tracy. Westport, Conn.: Auburn House.

Fraser, D. (1973) *The evolution of the British welfare state.* London: Macmillan.

Fields, F. and M. Owen (1993) *Private pensions for all: Squaring the circle.* London: Fabian Society.

Titmuss, R.M.T. (1958) The social divisions of welfare. In *Essays on the welfare state*, ed. R. Titmuss. London: Allen and Unwin, 34–55.

7

Indigenous Support and Social Security: Lessons from Kenya

Franz von Benda-Beckmann, Hans Gsänger, and James Midgley

Statutory social security programs have been created by governments not only in the industrial countries but in the developing countries of the so-called Third World as well. Social security programs were usually introduced into these countries in the period after World War II either by the former colonial powers or by international agencies, such as the International Labour Office, which actively promoted the growth of centrally administered insurance-funded programs in the newly independent nations.

The expansion of social security in the countries of the Third World was believed to be compatible with their efforts to become modern, industrial states. In the West, the evolution of social security was closely associated with the process of industrialization. As labor moved out of the agrarian subsistence economy into wage employment, the pressure to provide formal systems of social protection increased. Governments gradually created statutory social security schemes to meet the needs of those in wage employment. Eventually, the great majority of the population was covered by modern, statutory social security schemes.

Scholars such as Cockburn (1980) believed that similar trends would occur in the developing countries. It was recognized that social security would initially cater to only a relatively small proportion of the labor force employed in the modern sector of the economy, but as development drew

larger numbers of people out of the subsistence sector into the wage labor
sector, it was believed that social security would expand eventually to protect the majority of the population.

In the mean time, those who depended on agriculture for their livelihood would continue to be protected by indigenous social security institutions. In most societies, the indigenous system appeared to provide
adequate protection. It seemed that traditional family obligations and a
variety of other institutions insured that those in need were assisted. However, it was thought that the indigenous system would become less effective under the destructive influence of modernization. Changing family
norms, new attitudes, increased social mobility, and other factors would
eventually undermine traditional forms of support and thus require the
expansion of modern statutory programs.

While it is true that economic modernization has significantly altered
patterns of labor utilization in some developing countries, the prediction
that development would dramatically transform the developing countries
from agrarian to modern industrial states has not transpired. While many
countries have experienced significant growth in modern wage employment, the traditional rural agrarian sector has not been denuded. In addition, there has been rapid growth in the urban informal sector, which
appears to provide a more substantial locus for economic activities than
does the formal wage employment sector. Although there are exceptions,
economic modernization has not facilitated the extension of social security coverage to the mass of the population of developing countries. Instead, the proportion of citizens who are protected by statutory social
security in most Third World countries remains small, raising serious questions about the effectiveness as well as the equity of statutory social security
in these nations (Midgley, 1984).

Research into the extent of coverage by statutory social security programs in developing countries reveals that the proportion of the population covered by social security remains relatively small. Gruat (1990)
found that social security protection in Africa ranged from 1 percent of
the population in Chad, Gambia, and Niger to 22 percent in Egypt and
24 percent in Tunisia. When compared with figures published by Mouton
(1975) in the 1970s, Gruat's study suggests that the situation has only
improved marginally. Mesa-Lago (1992) reported that Latin American
countries such as Bolivia, Columbia, Ecuador, Guatemala, Nicaragua, and
Peru had coverage rates of less than a third of the labor force, while in
the Dominican Republic, El Salvador, Honduras, and Paraguay coverage
was less than 15 percent. Mesa-Lago's (1992) analysis of coverage rates in
Asia suggests that the situation in this region is also unsatisfactory. Only
8 percent of the labor force was protected by social security in India, while
in Thailand the figure was 10 percent; in Indonesia only 12 percent of
the labor force was covered. When compared with earlier research un-

dertaken by Thompson (1979), it seems that minimal improvements have taken place.

The recognition that economic development has not extended social security protection to the mass of the population has facilitated renewed interest in indigenous social security institutions. Social scientists such as Franz and Keebet von Benda-Beckmann and their colleagues (1988; 1994) have analyzed indigenous social security institutions and asked whether the indigenous system provides effective social protection. Some social policy analysts (Gilbert, 1976; Midgley, 1984, 1994) have considered the policy implications of this research, examining the role of governments in supporting the indigenous systems. They have argued that it is possible to integrate statutory social security with indigenous forms of social protection. Attempts to promote integration could, they believe, provide a workable alternative to conventional social insurance approaches, which have failed to provide social protection to the population as a whole. Through fostering integration, it may be possible to extend coverage and create a more effective and just system of social security suited to the needs of developing countries.

Policies and programs that integrate the indigenous social security and statutory systems can provide an alternative to conventional statutory approaches. In examining this issue, we employ case study material from Kenya, a developing country where policy research has been undertaken to address this issue (Gsänger, 1994). This research suggests that innovations can be introduced that will link the indigenous and statutory system to extend coverage to those who are currently excluded. In this chapter we also consider whether the experience of the developing countries can be of use to those in the industrial nations. Faced with aging populations, greater pressure on existing resources, and growing reluctance to increase revenues for social programs, policy makers in industrial nations may wish to consider alternatives that integrate non-statutory and statutory provisions. However, before discussing these issues, the nature of the indigenous social security system and the way it currently operates in Third World societies should be considered.

CHARACTERISTICS OF INDIGENOUS SOCIAL SECURITY

It is important that efforts to formulate policies for the integration of indigenous and statutory social security systems be founded on a proper understanding of how indigenous systems operate. Policies should be based on systematic research rather than intuitive beliefs and attitudes about traditional forms of support. Too often development policies and projects have failed to reach their objectives because they were based upon inadequate understandings of indigenous institutions.

For example, uninformed opinion about the indigenous system have tended toward two extreme positions, both of which are misleading. The pessimistic one maintains that traditional institutions are breaking down and have to be replaced, while the the the optimistic one avows that traditional institutions are good and function much better that statutory ones. The belief that traditional solidarity is breaking down does not tell us much about the enormous variation in the social security functions of contemporary indigenous social security, nor about the nature of changes in these functions. Although people may be poor and social relationships that in the past may have provided more social security have weakened, these relationships remain the primary vehicle through which people in need and distress receive at least some measure of help (World Bank, 1994). On the other hand, romantic visions of kinship solidarity are not justified either. Apart from a universal tendency toward individualization that reduces the scope of indigenous social security, kinship-based relations of mutual help sometimes collapse under extreme conditions. This has been observed where people were faced with severe drought and famine (Agarwal, 1991; de Bruijn and van Dijk, 1995).

More recent research has led to changed perspectives and policies toward nonstatutory and nonmarket social security arrangements. It is increasingly (though somewhat belatedly) realized that whatever strength contemporary arrangements of indigenous social security arrangements may have, the extension of statutory schemes or the introduction of innovative, integrative social security arrangements. Statutory programs should complement rather than substitute for indigenous systems (Benda-Beckmann 1994; World Bank, 1994).

Analytical perspectives on social security and policy options have also become more refined (Midgley, 1984, 1994; Ahmad, et al. 1991; von Benda-Beckmann, 1994). These analyses have shown that it is important to distinguish between the *mechanisms* and *conditions* of social security. Mechanisms are the normative and organizational framework through which resources are converted into actual social security provisions. Conditions for social security comprise the resources to be used in the provision of social security (Benda-Beckmann, 1994, Drèze and Sen, 1991). To a large extent, these resources are also part of social security mechanisms. But there is no direct relation between the availability of resources and the levels of welfare and security of people. These are mediated through relations of differential allocation and (re)distribution, at whatever level of socioeconomic organization. It holds true for the pooling of resources and redistribution of resources by government, as well as for relationships and transfers within groups of kin and communities. So while the distinction between conditions for and the mechanisms of social security is largely analytical and may sometimes be difficult to make empirically, it is important because the conditions for social security may be affected differently by changing economic, ecological, or political circumstances. They also have different implications for attempts to integrate indigenous and statutory social security. It is also important to distinguish "social security" from a "multilayered" functional perspective (Benda-Beckmann, 1994) that gives due attention to the different manifestations of social security at the layers of ideology, normative institutional framworks, and social relationships and social practices with their interrelationships. Conventional approaches that do not distinguish systematically between these layers lead to deducing social practices and actual social security provision from rules and procedures, or vice versa.

Generalizing statements and a priori assumptions cannot substitute for careful research on the actual conditions of indigenous social security mechanisms in the region or social domain for which one contemplates changes (Midgley, 1984, 1994; Benda-Beckmann, 1994). However, while generalizing statements must be avoided, it is important to make explicit those characteristics of indigenous social security institutions that are likely to shape the consequences of any new attempt to change them or integrate them with external organizations of social security and that on their part are likely to be affected in form and function by such innovations. Before the experience of Kenya is examined, the key characteristics of indigenous social security should be reviewed. As suggested earlier, policies that seek to integrate statutory and indigenous social security systems should be based on a sound understanding of these characteristics.

To understand indigenous forms of social security, it is important to recognize that indigenous social security consists of a variety of social relationships. The most frequent relationships are based on kinship, friendship, neighborhood, village membership, and patron-client interactions. These relationships are rarely differentiated from "ordinary" social and economic relationships. The same relationships serve normal life situations as well as periods of need and distress. Moreover, the social security dimension in these relationships is usually only one of many different aspects that are interwoven in complex social relationships. This means that these relationships are also multifunctional in that they may serve as a vehicle for social security provisions but may have other social, economic, or political functions as well. Also at the normative level, there is rarely a body of "social security" rules that is clearly set apart from general legal rules and principles for creating rights and obligations to provide help in categorically specified situations of need.

It is characteristic of these relationships that most people are both providers and recipients of social security. While the relation between receiving and providing usually changes with people's life cycles, they are most of the time providers and receivers. However, these relationships rarely are bilateral in the sense that they interconnect one person with another one, or with an institution or an agency in isolation. Provider-recipient relationships typically are embedded within a network of social relationships that interconnects a multitude of bilateral relations between a larger number of persons and institutions.

Another characteristic of indigenous social security is that it is based on social relationships that are clustered in a relatively small social and geographical space. Therefore, they have limited potential to provide a basis upon which resources can be pooled and redistributed on a wider social and geographical scale. They are also especially vulnerable to some specific forms of risks (Agawal, 1991; Platteau, 1991). However, this does not mean that they are wholly confined to small spaces. Rural-urban linkages are quite common, patron-client and kinship relationships may extend over wide geographical spaces and may even be intercontinental. Regional, national, and transnational migration may be very much part of local social security mechanisms. Remittances of migrant laborers from many parts of the world constitute an important source of provision of social security for those back home and lead to new and important forms of economic and social differentiation within the home communities (Brouwer, 1994; Böcker, 1994; Leliveld, 1994).

Another characteristic is that indigenous social security is based on complex mixes of mechanisms and provisions. Most people are involved in a multiplicity of social security relationships along which goods and services for their needs can be provided. To varying degrees, people have social security mixes that are based on a multiplicity of social relationships. These can be with kinsmen, friends, patrons, community functionaries, religious institutions, government bureaucracies, or commercial insurance enterprises.

This means that indigenous systems of social security do not exist in geographical or socioeconomic isolation. One cannot assume a complete absence of interconnections between the persons who are part of parallel systems. In most contemporary societies, there is already a plurality of normative orders, each with its own definition of needs and responsibilities. These provide different relationships through which social security can be provided. In fact, many individuals are participants in both indigenous and statutory systems. A considerable (and increasing) number of people in rural areas profit directly or indirectly from services provided by the state. State and local social security provision may come together on the basis of kinship or friendship relations or other forms of cooperation between civil servants and ordinary villagers. Civil servants, expecting to become dependent on their relatives in the future, may provide family members with help in the form of money or important services. This means that different social security mechanisms operating at different levels of social organization may merge in such social relationship or networks.

Finally, indigenous social security is characterized by dynamic processes. People try to maintain or rearrange their relations in changing circumstances, and they try to maintain existing relationships or to establish new relationships through which they hope to secure their well-being and that of their children and family members. But not everyone has the ability to draw on existing resources or to acquire new ones. People's social security mixes are specific to gender, age, class, and status. Whether and to what extent people are able to create and mobilize various options depends on many factors. Rights and relationships are important elements, but such rights rarely exist without concomitant, often reciprocal, obligations, which must have been fulfilled in the past or must be fulfilled in the future. Besides, the character of the relationships with potential providers of social security is very important. In particular, power and influence and command over economic resources are always important factors for gaining access to existing institutions and for establishing social security relations.

Social change continuously affects and reshapes these relationships. This pertains to interdependences among social relationships within the "indigenous" as well as between indigenous and statutory sectors. The growth of self-help groups and rotating savings and credit associations (ROSCAs) may significantly influence the scope and intensity of resource transfers within kinship networks. They reduce the amount of resources available for use within the family. New forms of social and economic integration achieved by these newly merged relationships and the changing allocation of resources that accompanies them often result in the disintegration of other relationhips and losses in the resources available to maintain them.

These features of indigenous social security should be kept in mind when attempts are made to integrate indigenous and statutory forms of social security. They will inform the case study material pertaining to Kenya where, it will be suggested, there is considerable potential for integrating different forms of social security.

INTEGRATING INDIGENOUS AND STATUTORY SOCIAL SECURITY: THE CASE OF KENYA

Only a small proportion of Kenya's 27 million people has access to modern forms of social protection. Most of them are in regular wage employment and they achieve a degree of protection from government and private forms of social security usually based on employment-related contributions. On the other hand, the vast majority of the population has to seek protection through a combination of individual provisions based on individual economic activities and traditional forms of solidarity, such as those provided through extended family, friendship, and community networks. Although they have sporadic links with modern social security and welfare facilities, the bulk of the population is dependent on the family or the community for help when in need.

Of about 11 million people who are gainfully employed, it is estimated that approximately 1.4 million have access to the country's statutory social security system. These schemes include the National Social Security Fund (NSSF), the National Hospital Insurance Fund (NHIF), and private provident funds and noncontributory pension schemes for civil servants and members of the armed forces.

The formal, statutory and the informal, traditional social security systems still operate as institutionally discrete subsystems. Somewhere in between are the self-organized, group-based social insurance schemes operated by trade unions, savings and credit cooperative societies, welfare associations and self-help groups.

The need to redesign the country's social protection system is evident for an increasing number of Kenyans are finding that social security is under threat from rapid processes of social and economic change. Economic problems based on limited access to productive resources, low productivity, and increasing levels of disguised and open unemployment are reducing the strengths and coping capacity of the country's social security systems. In addition, inappropriate development strategies have contributed to further losses of economic and social security for large numbers of people. These strategies include structural adjustment programs and an emphasis on high rates of economic growth without a concomitant emphasis on equity considerations.

To meet the social protection needs of the population, especially those of the poor and vulnerable, Kenya's formal social security institutions should be institutionally linked to the indigenous social system and the self-help initiatives of local groups and communities. This will not only increase social protection but enhance solidarity. Intergrating the country's various independently operating social security systems could make a significant contribution to alleviating the country's serious social problems.

Four Pillars of Indigenous Social Security in Kenya

The indigenous social security system as it exists in Kenya rests predominantly on four pillars. The first pillar is based on individual provisions derived from individual economic activities. Included in this category are the economic activities of self-employed peasants and subsistence farmers or casual wage laborers in agriculture. The second pillar consists of membership in traditional solidarity networks including the extended family and neighborhood units. The third pillar is comprised of membership in cooperative or social welfare associations such as self-help groups, rotating savings and credit associations (ROSCAs), and cultural groups. The last pillar is based on access to the benefits provided by nongovernmental voluntary organizations, churches, and trade unions.

However, these various forms of social security do not, as is sometimes maintained, provide adequate social protection for the whole population. Some forms of social security, such as that provided by the nongovernmental sector, do not cover the whole country and may be limited to certain groups, thus neglecting the needs of others.

Perhaps the most reliable source of social security is the traditional exchange system anchored in the nuclear and extended family. But in times of social and economic crises, when help is most needed, family members might themselves be destitute and unable to assist those seeking support. In addition, indigenous family-based social security in Kenya has been weakened by a squeeze on the productive resources families can command caused by land scarcity and other factors as well as a squeeze on incomes caused by structural adjustment programs, the imposition of cost-sharing in education and health, and inflation.

Traditional welfare associations and self-help groups play an increasingly important role in providing informal social protection. These organizations are an integral feature of Kenyan society and have also gained political prominence through the Harambee (cooperative) movement. There are tens of thousands of such associations, most of them unregistered, that enhance the economic and social security of their members. This is achieved through rotating savings and credit arrangements. Credit is provided by these associations for the purchase of household and investment goods, and for paying school and other fees. The associations also provide emergency funding in cases of sickness and hospitalization, death, and funerals. They also facilitate such income-generating activities as farming and marketing, running shops, and producing and selling handicrafts. While the more visible associations, which are registered with the Department of Social Services, are dominated by men, many others are run by women. The National Census of Women Groups in Kenya identified more than 23,000 women's groups with a total membership of almost a million persons.

In recent years, as economic and social conditions in Kenya have deteriorated, there has been accelerated growth in informal self-help groups. This is reported by various observers, including employees of foreign-aid agencies, church leaders, and academics. However, most also report that the effectiveness of self-help groups in enhancing social security varies widely. While some are successful and stable, others are ephemeral and of limited effectiveness. Nevertheless, the existence of these groups provides a basis for interlinking the indigenous and statutory systems and extending social protection to many more people.

In addition to the plethora of traditional welfare associations and self-help groups, there are also many formalized, nongovernmental organizations. These organizations are required to register under the government's Non-governmental Organization's (Registration) Act of 1991, and it is believed that between 400 and 500 such organizations currently exist. Many but not all of them are internationally funded and their fields of operations comprise a wide range of activities, including traditional social welfare services and poor relief. Much of their recent growth is a response to rising disillusionment about the government's capacity to efficiently deliver services. Growth has also been fueled by the increasing frustration of the international donor community with the inefficienc of government-run projects, which has resulted in a greater commitment among donors to nongovernmental organizations.

The nongovernmental and self-help sectors have played a more critical role in providing assistance to the poor in recent years as government subsidies and supports have been cut through the adoption of structural adjustment and related programs. Conventional social sector transfer payments were abolished without being replaced by an effective system of targeted transfers to the poor. The result has been increased poverty and destitution. The gap is today partially filled by self-help and voluntary social service programs managed by nongovernmental organizations.

Integrating Social Security Systems for Effective Protection

The present coverage of the formal social security system in Kenya is very limited, and the actual level of social protection it achieves is unsatisfactory both in terms of local standards and the minimum standards of the International Labour Organization. As was noted earlier, the majority of Kenyans have to rely on informal, indigenous social security arrangements that are today overburdened as a result of social and economic changes and the current economic crisis.

Since it is highly unlikely that the Kenyan economy will soon create a level of wage employment that will bring most or at least the majority of Kenyans into an employment-based formal social security system, new forms of provision based on appropriate social security policies must be developed. First, it is important to end the compartmentalization of the indigenous and statutory systems and approach social security with a holistic point of view. As Midgley (1994) urged, the dualism that characterizes current social security policy will only end when statutory and indigenous provisions are interlinked within the framework of a comprehensive policy for providing social protection for all.

If a stable social security system is to be created, various social security institutions should be linked so that each performs the tasks for which it is best suited. This idea is based on the concept of subsidiarity. In Kenya, the lowest viable level is the extended family, followed by traditional solidarity, and friendship and self-help groups. Above them are formal groups, such as cooperatives, nongovernmental associations of various kinds, churches, insurance companies, and, finally, governmental institutions.

The idea of the state acting on the subsidiarity principle also suggests that a reduction in central government involvement in the social sector is appropriate if it results in the emergence of community-based social security systems. These grass-roots systems could be planned and operated in close coordination with voluntary organizations. However, an appropriate legal framework is a prerequisite for a policy of this kind and some subsidization will be needed. Above all, the state should seek to foster a pluralistic but integrated and coordinated system of social security in which particular policy objectives for extending coverage can be pursued.

Within a comprehensive policy framework of this kind, a major objective should be to formalize the indigenous system so that those who are currently protected by indigenous forms of social security are given statutory recognition and support. Another major policy objective should be to extend the limited coverage of the statutory system to provide protection to those who are currently excluded.

With regard to the latter proposal, Gsänger (1994) proposed that the country's National Social Security Fund be modified to offer coverage to those in self-employment in the informal economy. However, such provision should be entirely voluntary since attempts to impose membership are likely to generate new problems, such as evasion that could be costly to remedy. A purely voluntary system of membership might appeal to small, individual and family-owed enterprises and might gradually result in greater coverage.

It is also important that steps be taken to remedy the equity problems that exist within the statutory system. The privileges that are currently enjoyed by civil servants who do not contribute to their retirement fund should be terminated, and a contributory system should be instituted. Similarly, efforts by the trade unions to introduce unemployment insurance for those who work in the wage-employment sector should be resisted. As Gsänger (1994: 27) pointed out, a scheme of this kind will, in the current economic climate, rapidly outstrip contributions, resulting in state subsidies to this group. To provide comparatively privileged wage earners with unemployment benefits that have been denied to more than 80 percent of the labor force is unacceptable.

Steps should also be taken to link the indigenous and formal systems by recognizing and formalizing the social security practices of traditional welfare and self-help associations. Empirical observations in Kenya and in other parts of the developing world, such as India and Bangladesh, reveal that these organizations are quite capable of making innovative and appropriate contributions to social security. However, they have finite physical and monetary resources and therefore deserve assistance from the government. Although there are as yet very few examples of successful interlinking programs of this kind, there is no doubt that these organizations are able to provide social security when they are given appropriate support within an amenable political and legal environment. In many countries, formal voluntary associations have shown that they are able to utilize the support provided by government in a highly effective way.

One way of building social security capacity would be to federate grassroot groups into larger associations that could provide group insurance coverage to their constituent member groups. However, such efforts must insure full participation of members. Often they fail when they do not address the priority needs of their beneficiaries. In this regard, it is vital that governments do not seek to control or overregulate self-help and nongovernmental organizations. The involvement of these groups in social security will be enhanced by avoiding overbureaucratization and by fostering participation and democratic decision making.

To promote the involvement of these associations in social security, governments should provide subsidies, technical assistance, and training. Attention should also be given to fostering group cohesion and insuring that the composition of these associations is balanced. Effective social security associations will have a healthy balance between economically active and nonactive group members. This is an important determinant of a group's social security capacity. Another important factor is group stability. Social relations within the group and group cohesion need to be stable and dependable. Finally, groups need to have recognized rules of distribution. Specific rules should be put in place for identifying needy members and distributing goods and services to them.

In the day-to-day business of self-help promotion, attention must also be given to promoting the efficiency of voluntary social security organizations. Management problems, high administrative costs, irregularities, and uncertainties threaten the effectiveness of self-help organizations. From time to time, even church organizations report cases of embezzlement and a self-service mentality. Yet, as in the public sector, some transparency in the conduct of management and funding can be ensured if a proper climate for efficient and accountable management is created. Government has a major role to play in this regard.

In addition to these specific measures for promoting the linking of the statutory and indigenous social security system, the government needs to adopt policies and programs that address the basic social and economic needs of citizens. It is vitally important that efforts be made to insure the stabilization of the livelihood of poor population groups. Current economic and social policies need to be critically reviewed in light of their social impact. There is little point in trying to enhance the effectiveness of the social security system if wider social and economic policies exacerbate the conditions of poverty and deprivation that continue to characterize the lives of millions of people in Kenya and other developing countries.

CONCLUSION: RELEVANCE TO THE INDUSTRIAL NATIONS

Research into the indigenous social security sector in Kenya has resulted in several policy proposals that could foster the integration of formal, statutory schemes with traditional forms of social support. This research has obvious relevance to other developing countries in which statutory social security schemes with limited coverage coexist with larger, indigenous systems. However, it is also relevant to social security policy in the industrial nations. It is today more widely recognized that the industrial nations have much to learn from the developing countries. The idea that the developing countries are less advanced and that they should, therefore, emulate the experiences of the industrial nations has been widely discredited. Instead, it is now being proposed that policy innovations should be transferred in both directions and that truly reciprocal exchanges between the industrial and developing countries should be fostered. As will be shown, social security policy in the industrial countries can benefit from the debates that have taken place in the Third World about integrating indigenous and statutory social security.

In the years following World War II, it was widely accepted that governments should be the primary provider of social welfare services. The adoption of New Deal social programs in the United States, the election of social democratic political parties in many European countries, and the expansion of government involvement in social welfare in many parts of the world reinforced the principles of welfare statism. Despite the fact that voluntary and self-help associations remained active, it was widely believed that governments would eventually replace these nonstatutory forms of provision and that social welfare would ultimately be the responsibility of the modern state.

Today the situation has changed dramatically. Economic difficulties, electoral resistance, and the rise of radical right-wing ideological movements have slowed the expansion of government social programs in the West and undermined the assumptions on which welfare statism are based. Instead, welfare pluralism is today recognized not only as an inevitable fact but as a preferred basis for social welfare. Most political parties, including those that championed government intervention in social welfare, now accept the desirability of a pluralistic welfare system in which diverse sources of provision coexist to cater to the needs of citizens.

Accordingly, the contribution of the voluntary sector in the industrial countries is more widely recognized, and governments more frequently contract with these organizations to provide services that were previously delivered by government bureaucracies themselves. Commercial providers of social welfare services have also expanded, particularly in the United States, and these firms now regularly compete for government contracts to supply social services on a for-profit basis.

In addition, research into informal forms of social security has increased, and it is today widely recognized that families, neighbors, and friends are major providers of social welfare. The implications of this research have not been fully developed, but there has been a tendency in policy circles to assume that social needs can be effectively met by devolving responsibility for care to relatives and local communities. Unfortunately, the transfer of responsibility to nonformal care networks has not always been accompanied by adequate budgetary and other forms of support, with the result that family members have often been faced with heavy additional responsibilities that have severely strained their resources. In addition, deinstitutionalization and a reduction in the availability of residential services have not been replaced with adequate community-based services, with the result that the social needs of client groups have not been adequately met. In view of these problems, many social policy experts have concluded that more research into nonformal social security is needed and that its contribution must be more carefully assessed.

It is unfortunate that discussions of the role of nonformal social welfare systems in the industrial countries have ignored the growing literature on the subject emanating from the Third World, where indigenous systems of support are well developed and extensively used. As the case study material presented in this chapter reveals, numerous policy recommendations have emerged from this research. These recommendations are equally relevant to the industrial countries.

For example, the recommendation that indigenous forms of social security in the Third World need to be properly harmonized with statutory and voluntary forms of provision is equally relevant to the industrial countries. However, there is little evidence that steps have been taken to foster the emergence of a comprehensively planned, pluralistic welfare system in these countries. Instead, the principle of subsidiarity is often implemented on an ad hoc basis, fostering a fragmented and ineffective system of provision. This problem is particularly evident in the United States, where, as Karger and Stoesz (1994: 19) pointed out, the welfare system is often referred to as a "welfare mess." Efforts in the developing countries to foster integration should be examined by Western social policy experts and adapted for local use.

Other recommendations emanating from research into indigenous social security systems in the developing countries can be equally useful for policy formulation in the industrial nations. By learning from the Third

World, policy makers in the West can refine proposals, anticipate problems, and enhance the effectiveness of their interventions.

REFERENCES

Ahmad, A. (1991) et al., eds. (1991) *Social security in developing countries.* Oxford: Clarendon Press.

Argawal, B. (1991) Social security and the family: Coping with seasonality and calamity in rural India. In eds. A. Ahmad, et al. *Social security in developing countries.* Oxford: Clarendon Press, 171–244.

Benda-Beckmann, F. von, et al. (1988) Introduction: Between kinship and the state. In *Between kinship and the state: Social security and law in developing countries,* eds. F. von Benda-Beckmann, et al. Dordrecht, the Netherlands: Foris Publications, 7–20.

Benda-Beckmann, F. von (1988) Islamic law and social security in an Ambonese village. In *Between kinship and the state: Social security and law in developing countries,* eds. F. von Benda-Beckmann, et al. Dordrecht, the Netherlands: Foris Publications, 339–66.

Benda-Beckmann, F. von (1994) Coping with Insecurity. *Focaal* 22/23(1): 7–34.

Böcker, A. (1994) *Turkse migranten en sociale zekerheid: Van onderlinge zorg naar overheidszorg?* Amsterdam: Amsterdam University Press.

Brouwer, R. (1994) Insecure at home: Emigration and social security in northern portugal. *Focaal* 22/23(1): 153–75.

Bruijn, M. de and H. van Dijk (1995) *Arid ways: Cultural understandings of insecurity in Fulbe society, central Mali.* Amsterdam: Thesis Publishers.

Braun, J. von (1991) Social security in Sub-Saharan Africa: Reflections on policy changes. In *Social Security in Developing Countries* eds. E. Ahmad, et al. Oxford: Clarendon Press, 395–414.

Cockburn, C. (1980) The role of social security in development. *International Social Security Review* 33(4): 337–58.

Drèze, J. and A. Sen. (1991) Public action for social security. In eds. A. Ahmad, et al. *Social security in developing countries.* Oxford: Clarendon Press, 1–40.

Getubig, I. P. (1992) Non-conventional forms of social security protection for the poor in Asia. In *Rethinking social security: Reaching out to the poor,* eds. I. P. Getubig and Sonke Schmidt. Kuala Lumpur, Malaysia: Asian and Pacific Development Centre, 106–35.

Gilbert, N. (1976) Alternative forms of social protection for developing countries. *Social Security Review* 50(4): 363–87.

Gruat, J. V. (1990) Social security schemes in Africa: Current trends and problems. *International Labour Review* 129(4): 405–21.

Gsänger, H. (1994) *Social security and poverty in Kenya: Developing social security systems for poverty alleviation.* Berlin: GDI.

Gsänger H. and P. Waller (1993) *Perspektiven der deutschen Entwicklungszusammenarbeit mit der Republik Kenia.* Berlin: GDI.

Guhan, S. (1994) Social security options for developing countries. *International Labour Review* 133(1): 35–53.

International Labour Office and United Nations Development Program (1992) *Development of social security: Kenya.* Draft Project Report. Nairobi: International Labour Office and United Nations Development Program.

Kanyinga, K. (1993) The socio-political context of the growth of non-governmental organizations in Kenya. In *Social change and economic reform in africa,* ed. P. Gibbon. Uppsala, Sweden: Scandinavian Institute of African Studies, 70–82.

Karger, H. and D. Stoesz (1994) *American social welfare policy.* New York:, Longman.

Kenya and United Nations Children's Fund (1992) *Children and women in Kenya: A situation analysis.* Nairobi: Government of Kenya and UNICEF.

Leliveld, A. (1994) *Social security in developing countries: Operation and dynamics of social security in rural Swaziland.* Amsterdam: Tinbergen Institute Research Series no. 85.

Mesa-Lago, C. (1992). Comparative analysis of Asia and Latin American social security Systems. In *Rethinking social security: Reaching out to the poor,* eds. I. P. Getubig and Sonke Schmidt. Kuala Lumpur, Malaysia: Asian and Pacific Development Centre, 64–105.

Midgley, J. (1984) *Social security, inequality and the Third World.* Chichester, England: Wiley.

Midgley, J. (1994) Social security policy in developing countries: Integrating state and traditional systems. *Focaal* 22/34(1): 219–30.

Mouton, P. (1975) *Social security in Africa: Trends, problems and prospects.* Geneva: International Labour Office.

Ngau, N. (1994) *A survey of household welfare, income status and survival strategies in Mathare Valley.* Draft Report. Nairobi: GTZ.

Platteau, J.P. (1991) "Traditional systems of social security and hunger insurance: Achievements and Modern challenges." In eds. A. Ahmad, et al. *Social security in developing countries.* Oxford: Clarendon Press, pp. 112–70.

Thompson, K. (1979) Trends and problems of social security in developing countries in Asia. In *The role of trade unions in social security: Report of a regional seminar.* Bangkok: International Labour Officer, 109–44.

World Bank (1994) *Averting the old age crisis: Policies to protect the old and promote growth.* Washington, D.C.: The World Bank.

8

Conclusion: Social Security in the Twenty-first Century

Michael Sherraden

The diverse examples of social security in the preceding chapters give us much to consider. Foremost, these examples leave us with an understanding that there is no single best way to provide social protection. The alternatives are numerous and varied, and combinations of different types of social security can and often do work side by side within a single country. In general, the most constructive approach is to think of social security not as a monolithic system, but as a combination of policies that are mutually complementary. In the language of the influential and controversial report of the World Bank (1994), we should think of social security not as a single pillar, but as multiple pillars. This "pillars" language suggests that each leg of the system should bear more or less equal weight, which I think is open to discussion, but the idea of multiple strategies within a single country is well taken. In the current U.S. environment of rather simplistic policy positions—either total support for the existing social security system or total opposition to it—acknowledgment in public debate of multiple alternatives and combinations of policy approaches would be a welcome step forward.

OPTIONS IN SOCIAL SECURITY POLICY

The list of alternatives in social security policy covers a wide ideological and practical spectrum. Proceeding from the more market oriented to the more state interventionist, basic policy options include the following:

private charity (with tax incentives): donations by individuals or corporations for charitable purposes.

non-profit services and provisions (with tax incentives): services and protections organized through churches, and social service and other non-profit organizations.

corporate or occupational provisions (with tax incentives): services and protections organized through employers.

"privatized" social security (with tax incentives): individual accounts regulated by the state but managed by the participant and investment companies.

provident fund (with tax incentives): individual accounts managed by the state.

social assistance: means-tested transfers from general revenues to the poor.

social insurance: contributory defined-benefit public programs.

social allowance (or demogrant): universal grants from general revenues.

social provision (in a lesser form, price subsidy): free or reduced price goods and services.

This list begins with limited state responsibility and moves toward more comprehensive state responsibility, a continuum that is useful in defining political ideologies and practical choices. The Right has typically preferred policies near the top of the list, while the Left has preferred policies near the bottom. The Right has assumed that the efficiency of private markets and the motivation of individual citizens are distorted by state interventions, and therefore less state intervention is preferred. The Left has assumed that the political state should be a counterweight to hardship, inequality, and other negative outcomes of the market, and therefore more state intervention is preferred. Throughout the twentieth century, the Left has sometimes articulated a neo-Marxist theme in its social security thinking, wherein the welfare state is viewed as a path toward socialism. This is sometimes presented as a natural progression, as in T. H. Marshall's (1964) view of the evolution of social rights. But the examples in this volume do not lend much support to the idea that one form of social security is a natural predecessor or precursor to another. Indeed, one of the major lessons of the twentieth century is that different forms of social security can come and go in almost any order and combination.

Emphasis on Partnerships

The above list of social security options suggests that many creative partnerships in social security are possible, and indeed are often desirable.

Although analysts of social security tend to think of policy as something that is carried out by the political state, in fact, as the examples in this book clearly demonstrate, there are many complementary actors. The key actors in social policy are (1) the family, (2) friends and informal relationships, (3) the voluntary or nonprofit sector, (4) the commercial sector, and (5) the state. If one were to ask a sample of people to rank these five actors according to importance in providing social well-being or social security, only a small minority would list the state first. (I have carried out this exercise with students in the United States and in Singapore and "the state" typically ranks fourth or fifth in importance in both countries. I suspect that the ranking would not be much different in other countries, nor is it likely to be much different for elderly populations, despite the fact that they receive considerable financial support from the state in many countries.) What this suggests is that those of us who think about social policy would do well to broaden our view about the definition of policy consists, and who the key actors are. Especially, we should envision social policy that builds on the strengths of families, informal relationships, the voluntary sector, and the commercial sector. Some key questions are: Does each sector perform particular or unique social functions, and if so, what are these and how can they be supported? To what extent do the sectors work together, and what are the mechanisms of cooperation among sectors? What can the state do to augment, rather than replace, other forms of support?

The Rise of Defined Contribution Principles

In terms of overall content, the most striking trend in social security policy is the emergence of defined contribution principles, that is, the creation of asset accounts in which workers save and invest a portion of their earnings in an individual fund. Among the examples in this book, the trend toward defined contribution principles is most pronounced in Singapore and Chile, but it is also occurring in Australia, and there are recommendations for expansion of the system in the United Kingdom. Overall, defined contribution systems appear to be standing beside or replacing defined benefit systems as the dominant policy instrument in a large number of countries. For example, Mexico is making similar changes, and other Latin American countries, including Columbia, Peru, and Argentina, are doing the same (Ruiz Durán, forthcoming).

The distinction between defined benefit and defined contribution principles is the most fundamental policy issue at the micro or household level. Defined benefit systems, represented most notably by social insurance, offer guaranteed incomes in retirement—at least so long as the systems remain solvent. In theory, defined benefit systems also embrace solidarity principles, transferring resources from the well-off to the impoverished, although in practice the degree of solidarity varies greatly from country to country. On the other hand, defined contribution systems offer a greater sense of ownership, control, and flexibility in investing and using social security funds. The evidence from the Singapore chapter indicates that this control and flexibility can have many positive effects.

Funded vs. Pay-as-you-go

Turning to macro policy matters, the most fundamental distinction is whether the social security system is funded or pay-as-you-go (PAYG). This distinction is somewhat underemphasized in the chapters, and some of the chapters also do not emphasize the important age-related features of late twentieth-century social policy: the extent to which domestic policy expenditures go to households of the elderly (at the expense of households with children) and the rapidly aging populations of most countries. These benefit patterns and population pressures will bring increasing fiscal strain to PAYG social security systems.

Policy Change and the Search for New Formulations

Another prominent contribution of these policy examples is that social security systems can and sometimes do undergo massive changes in order to respond to a crisis or prepare for the future. Almost by definition, social security systems are large and deeply entrenched, but examples of comprehensive policy change in countries such as Australia, Hong Kong, and Chile indicate that embarking on new pathways is possible, both practically and politically. The clear lesson is that we should not presume that social security is a policy "too big to change" or "politically untouchable." What looks large and untouchable today may look very fluid and adaptive tomorrow.

COUNTRY-BY-COUNTRY NOTES

Australia

Rosenman outlined Australia's unique blend of social assistance and superannuation. The latter is a system of tax-advantaged savings for retirement, operating on defined contribution principles, with government tax benefits and privately managed funds. Superannuation, introduced in 1992, has two tiers, compulsory and contributory. The goals of superannuation are, over the long term, to reduce reliance on social assistance and raise capital for investment. Upon retirement, the superannuation can be taken as a lump sum, which is very popular, or as an annuity, which the government is trying to encourage through tax incentives. Despite

Rosenman's misgivings, it seems quite possible that in the long run the superannuation system will make the vast majority of Australians more secure in their old age, and also make the economy more productive through capital accumulation and increased investment.

The impetus for this policy change was concern about paying the broad, albeit shallow, social assistance (or age pension) to an aging population that is increasingly out of the labor market. The long-term aim of the new policy is to significantly replace the age pension. However, as the author noted, this may present a threat to low-wage earners, women, and others who have not accumulated very much in superannuation accounts. Under the age pension system, there was little stigma because there were so many recipients. But what happens, asked Rosenman, if there are eventually only a small number of age pension recipients? Will they be stigmatized? Will their benefits be vulnerable to political and budgetary pressures? These questions are fundamental to consideration of any backup means-tested system. The answers, I am afraid, are not very encouraging: we know from long experience in the United States and elsewhere that means-tested backups are likely to be inadequate, stigmatized, and politically vulnerable. The best policy solution is to bring as many people as possible into the primary system—through state subsidies if necessary—to avoid reliance on means-tested backups. However, Australia does not yet appear ready to do this. The larger point is that under any circumstances no single system will be enough. Some type of backup provisions will be needed for filling gaps for the most disadvantaged, regardless of the coverage and adequacy of the primary system.

Rosenman rightly noted that social assistance is not appropriate as a primary system where disposable income is high and reasonably distributed, and the population is aging. Under these circumstances, she recommended the traditional welfare state solution of social insurance. It is possible, however, that Australia is now on a more stable and sustainable policy path than are many countries with social insurance systems. Only time will determine whether or not this is the case.

Singapore

No Western nation would wish to adopt Singapore's heavy-handed and intrusive government policies. On the other hand, there may be some things that we can learn from Singapore that can be adapted to Western traditions. In this regard, the Central Provident Fund offers several possible lessons. The first is that a social security system can be built predominantly on asset accounts, and this simple structure can have multiple purposes. It is a flexible and adaptive mechanism; as capital accumulates and new conditions arise, new social security and social development purposes can be added. The policy is thus integrative at the household level,

with households choosing how much money to devote to housing, retirement, education, and so on. The policy is also integrative at the macro
level; it avoids the welfare state model of multiple, disconnected
categorical programs, each with its own bureaucracy. Although Singapore
has a considerable way to go in making the system universal by subsidizing
accounts for the poor, it has begun to take steps in this direction.

The Singapore government controls CPF wealth, which is, on a per
capita basis, a vast accumulation. To date, the government has reportedly
been a proficient manager of these funds (data are not available to con-
firm this), but with a highly centralized political system, Singaporeans are
concerned about eventual corruption, mismanagement, or both. Indeed,
this is the main reason that provident funds in the Singaporean sense
would not be a viable solution for most countries. The Chilean model of
investments in the private markets, like 401(k)s and individual retirement
accounts (IRAs) in the United States, will be much more suitable for most
countries that choose defined contribution systems. This is especially true
for countries with already well-developed capital markets.

Hong Kong

Hong Kong has bucked late twentieth-century trends in social policy by
affirming a social allowance (demogrant) scheme for old age. The social
allowances are universal, noncontributory pensions that begin at age seventy. As a complement, social assistance is available to the poor from ages
sixty-five to sixty-nine.

During the late 1980s and early 1990s, there was an active discussion in
Hong Kong regarding social security options. Social insurance was considered but was opposed by the Hong Kong business community and young
professionals, who preferred a defined contribution system. Along these
lines, it is also interesting that Hong Kong rejected the provident fund
model of its neighbor city-state of Singapore. Provident fund proposals
were rejected in 1987 and again in 1991. I have been told informally by
several parties that this was in large measure because of Chinese control
beginning in 1997 and fears that the Chinese government might in one
manner or another deplete the accumulated capital in a provident fund.

As Tang observed, we can learn from the example of Hong Kong that
a social allowance scheme is not necessarily a progression from social insurance, but instead can be a substitute for it. This is one more example
of a social security system "going its own way," responding to real world
conditions rather than to theoretical notions or prescribed pathways in
policy development.

Administratively, a social allowance scheme is relatively easy to implement and operate. Benefits can go directly to personal bank accounts.
Because the system is universal and everyone is treated the same, there is

limited record keeping, verification, and monitoring of eligibility or benefit amounts. Politically, the universal allowance tends to offset divisions in society; everyone is treated the same. These are major policy advantages. The social allowance also can be easily "harmonized" with other social security approaches.

Chile

A main theme of Borzutzky's chapter is that policy change toward "privatized" social security in Chile was possible only because of the authoritarian regime. This point is well taken, but there are other times when the author seemed to downplay the fact that the former Chilean social insurance system, like virtually all social insurance systems in Latin America, never did include lower-income workers, most of whom were not in the formal economy and thus were nonparticipants in social security. The author also downplayed the financial crisis of the old system; like many social insurance systems in Latin America, it was bankrupt and unsustainable.

To be sure, the new Chilean system based on individual asset accounts is far from perfect. There are, as in the old system, questions about coverage and adequacy for lower-income workers. Many workers will have very little in retirement benefits. These inadequacies may or may not diminish over time, depending upon whether more workers are brought into the formal economy. If the Chilean system is eventually to provide universal security, ways will have to be found to build asset accounts of everyone, including those who are not working. The current system is a long way from reaching this goal.

Nonetheless, the asset-based system is popular among most Chilean workers. Despite the radical nature of the change, there is relatively little opposition to it. Borzutzky understated the positive impacts at both household and macro levels, and also significantly understated the keen, though not uncritical, interest in the Chilean social security experience among other Latin America countries (see Ruiz Durán, forthcoming), as well as growing interest in the Chilean sytem among the welfare states in Europe and North America.

Britain

Owen and Field proposed that the existing state social insurance system be augmented by supplemental private occupational pensions in the form of compulsory savings in individual accounts. Those who are not able to contribute to savings accounts would receive deposits subsidized by the state. Owen and Field astutely observed the desirability of fully portable occupational benefits in a changing labor market. This defined contribution tier would be accompanied by educational programs on how to use the new accounts.

In effect, this would be an extension of the existing two-tier social security system to the whole population. The proposal is both practical and bold. It strongly embraces progressive principles, yet recognizes the success—both at micro and macro levels—of the existing occupational pension scheme, and seeks to build on this success.

Kenya

The chapter on Kenya by Benda-Beckmann, Gsänger, and Midgley is one of the most creative in the book, looking at indigenous patterns of family, community, and nongovernmental organization support as a system of security that should be complemented, rather than replaced by, statutory actions on the part of the state. As Midgley (1996) pointed out, the so-called developed nations may have much to learn from policy and practice models in developing nations, where the primary emphasis is development (rather than maintenance, which is the primary emphasis of welfare states). Developmental social policy emphasizes growth, change, and progress rather than consumption support. This approach to social policy would build on the work of organizations such as cooperatives, revolving savings and credit societies, self-help organizations, churches, and civic associations. This thinking has something in common with social policy proposals currently recommended in the United States by "bleeding heart conservatives" such as Jack Kemp and Senator Dan Coats and by "new Democrats" such as Senators Joseph Lieberman and John Breaux, wherein state resources are viewed as leverage for empowering local organization and community development.

This chapter opens many worthwhile considerations in social policy, but it also raises more questions than it answers. Foremost, how are linkages between local organizations and the state to be established and nurtured so that a coherent system emerges? What is the appropriate role of the state in such a system, and what specifically should the state do? What are the key policy tools? What evidence do we have that these might be effective?

SOCIAL POLICY IN THE TWENTIETH CENTURY: A CREATION OF INDUSTRIALISM

Looking back, the industrial era has been a "mass" era. We have assumed that a mass society can be sustained in low-skill employment that is essentially stable over the long term. At the household level, the assumption has been that most people will have a long-term job, and social security policy can, as necessary, supplement the income from this job.

In the industrial era, the basic idea of domestic policy has been to have an industrial economy that is productive enough so that it can be taxed to provide income—which is assumed to be roughly equivalent to consumption—for groups that do not receive sufficient income from the market economy. These groups typically include the retired, the disabled, the unemployed, dependent children, and sometimes others. Not every country has had the same policies, but the overall pattern has been that social insurance is the dominant income distribution mechanism. (It might be added that what is called "social insurance" is often not true insurance because the total benefits paid often far exceed the total premiums collected. In other words, the "insurance" benefits are in large part a transfer from general revenues, in effect an intergenerational welfare transfer.) The choice of social insurance as the dominant social security policy in the twentieth century is derived from certain assumptions and perspectives concerning industrialism and low-skill mass production. These assumptions are as follows:

Economies and labor markets are essentially closed and tied to nation-states. Therefore it makes sense to think exclusively in terms of national social policies that serve a nation's population.

Social and economic issues are and should remain almost completely separate. Indeed, the two are viewed as conflicting because resources are drawn away from production for individual and household consumption.

There is a preoccupation with mass problems and deficiencies, or "needs." These mass needs are addressed via categorical programs, which are centralized and operate as bureaucratic organizations. Bureaucracy is also a creation of the industrial era.

The unemployed require only income support when they are not earning labor income. In this regard, unemployment insurance is the epitome of industrial-era social security thinking: it provides income support with little emphasis on retraining for new employment. The assumption is that any unemployed person can take the next low-skill job that is available.

Retirement is a fixed period of inactivity late in life, a reward for several decades of hard physical labor. In fact, mass retirement was created by industrialism and the social policies that accompanied it. Prior to industrialism, most people worked until they were no longer able to do so.

AN ASSESSMENT OF SOCIAL POLICY IN THE WELFARE STATES

The twentieth-century welfare state was a remarkable and successful social innovation in its time. During the industrial era, the welfare state has lifted millions of people, especially the elderly, out of poverty. But industrial era policies have not been perfect, and time does not stand still. As the economy and social conditions change, PAYG income-based social policy is less and less functional to the world in which we live. Several general criticisms can be made about social security systems in the world today:

In terms of social protection, most social security systems have not been very progressive. The welfare state has largely served the middle class, while the poor have been second-class participants. This is particularly true in Latin America, where social security systems have tended to serve primarily the unionized labor force. A related point is that mass organized labor, which is also a feature of the industrial era, has not been deeply concerned about the conditions of the poor. To be sure, organized labor uses social justice rhetoric, but its actions tend to be on behalf of better-paid workers. To take a recent example, the 1995 French strike over reductions in welfare benefits was primarily on behalf of government workers seeking to protect their comfortable state pensions.

Income-based policy promotes consumption. The policy is designed almost exclusively to support consumption rather than savings. The macroeconomic effect is reduced domestic savings, reduced investment, and resulting slower growth and dependence on foreign capital.

Centralized cash payments in social security policy tend to undermine intrafamily and community support, not only in traditional societies, but in industrial nations as well. This "conservative" critique is essentially correct but is often unacknowledged by progressive policy analysts.

There are national boundary problems in an increasingly global economy. For example, to integrate the economies of the European Community (EC), labor migration and social security policy present major challenges. At present, large-scale labor migration from one country to another is unlikely because the EC has failed to harmonize social benefits from one country to another. Social security conditions differ so widely that they are a major impediment to mobility in a unified labor market.

Most social insurance systems today face serious fiscal problems. Pronounced demographic changes—the growing elderly population and declining birth rate—render almost all PAYG social insurance policies unsustainable in their current form (Japan may be a notable exception, due to rather impressive long-term planning). Fiscal crises have already occurred in many countries and are looming in others.

STRAIN IN WELFARE STATES

The history of welfare states was characterized, up to the 1980s, by periodic political struggles and the gradual expansion of benefits. These struggles and the hard-won expansion of benefits can be viewed as victories of caring over indifference. However, by the 1980s most large industrialized nations were facing severe fiscal strain. Because social welfare benefits had become half or more of national budgets in many countries, welfare spending became a target of discontent. This discontent contributed to the emergence of right-wing political regimes in some nations (notably the United States and the United Kingdom), and these regimes marshaled political opposition to welfare benefits—more particularly benefits oriented toward the poor (Glennerster and Midgley, 1991).

However, the vast bulk of welfare state spending does not go to the poor, but rather to the middle class. Right-wing regimes have had limited impact on the largest welfare provisions, notably retirement income and subsidized health care. Spending in these areas has continued to increase and, given aging populations, spending is projected to increase further in the years ahead. Strain on public budgets, already severe in the United States, Germany, Sweden, and many other countries, will likely become worse. Indeed, it is the hard reality of this fiscal strain, rather than right-wing political rhetoric, that is likely to cut into future welfare state spending. Signs of moderation in welfare spending for the middle class have appeared in France, Sweden, and Germany, and the United States may not be far behind. Unless there are major policy changes, Social Security Retirement, the largest U.S. social expenditure, will be in financial crisis around 2012, when benefits paid out will exceed receipts coming in— because the Social Security Trust Fund exists only on paper. And Medicare, the second largest social expenditure, will be in financial crisis around the year 2002.

In the United States, we have seen strong political reaction against any political party that raises these issues for discussion. Social Security has been the "third rail" of American politics, a reference to the electricity-carrying rail of a mass transit system—touch it and die. But this political reality will shift completely when a majority of the working population believes that it will not be collecting much social security but is still required to pay for the retirement benefits of the elderly. When this occurs, no politician will be able to avoid talking about reforms in Social Security.

Thus, Western welfare states have very likely reached a turning point. Questions are being raised about the very assumptions underlying the twentieth-century welfare state. During coming decades, it is likely that domestic policy in the West will undergo fundamental transformations.

WORLDWIDE TRENDS IN SOCIAL POLICY

In fact, as we have seen from some of the examples in this book, traditional welfare state policy has begun to change in the last years of the twentieth century. Trends in the world are as follows:

Reductions in means-tested support for the poor. This has occurred largely because spending for the poor is politically the easiest to cut. In this regard, it is ironic that relatively generous social insurance payments to the middle class are often defended by progressives on grounds of "solidarity" and "social justice," while the fiscal strain created by these entitlements often leads to reductions in spending on the poor.

A weakening in the dominance of defined-benefit social insurance. As fiscal strain increases, nations are turning to other forms of social protection to complement social insurance.

More mixed systems or multiple pillars in social security policy, as recommended in the 1994 report by the World Bank.

A rise in the use of asset-based policy in the form of individual accounts. These accounts are typically facilitated by public tax incentives for household savings. Several trends suggest that the emergence of this policy mechanism is widespread: (1) The success of national provident funds in Singapore and Malaysia has influenced the development of provident funds in the Pacific Islands, and Singapore is likely to have a major influence on Chinese social security policy. (2) The Chilean experience with privatized capital accounts is being copied to some extent by Argentina, Peru, Colombia, and several other Latin American countries. This widespread policy change in Latin America, although not yet "on the radar" of many U.S. policy analysts, is almost revolutionary in scope and impact—perhaps the most profound policy change on a single continent since the creation of the welfare state in Western Europe. (3) In the United States, we see a pronounced shift to defined contribution systems in the private sector; increasing proposals to make part of Social Security retirement a defined contribution system; and movement toward asset accumulation by the poor by raising means-tested asset limits, and creating Individual Development Accounts (IDAs), which are matched savings accounts for home owning, education, microenterprise, and other development purposes.

LOOKING TO THE FUTURE: THE IMPACT OF THE INFORMATION AGE

From our perspective around the year 2000, it is challenging to imagine what the world will be like even 100 years from now in 2100. For example, looking back to the United States in 1900, almost no one could have imagined that a hundred years hence in 2000 less than 2 percent of the labor force would be employed in agriculture. If someone had made such a prediction, he or she would have been ridiculed as wildly imaginative and unrealistic. This example is useful because it seems quite possible that by 2100 less than 2 percent of the U.S. labor force will be employed in industrial production—and the same may be true for almost every other country as well. This prediction may be perceived as unrealistic by many people; yet there is reason to believe that changes of historic magnitude are underway. Just as the agricultural era gave way to the industrial era; the industrial era is now giving way to the information era. Moreover, it seems likely that the information revolution will occur more rapidly and be more global in scope than the industrial revolution. Already, for example, there are internet connections to impoverished rural villages in India that have been virtually untouched by the industrial age. Within a few decades, it is possible that almost the entire world will be electronically interconnected.

We are on the front end of a massive technological transformation and the possible implications are almost breathtaking. Of particular interest regarding the discussion in this book, the information revolution will profoundly alter the way in which we perceive and carry out social security policy. In the long term, the following simple relationships are dominant:

Technology shapes economic organization.

Economic organization shapes social issues.

Social issues shape the policy responses of the state.

These are not new observations. These simple relationships were the underlying theme—and perhaps the most important intellectual contribution—of Karl Marx (1867), and they have been repeated in various forms by a wide range of economists, sociologists, and policy analysts throughout the twentieth century. As information technology reshapes economic organization, we will live through major—and often chaotic—social changes. These will, in turn, dramatically reshape social security policy. The thinking and solutions of yesterday will not be applicable in the world as it unfolds in the decades ahead.

ECONOMIC AND SOCIAL CHANGES THAT ARE LIKELY TO ACCOMPANY THE INFORMATION REVOLUTION

It is impossible to know exactly what economic and social conditions will be like by the end of the next century, but the following seem likely:

A more global economy, with stronger global and regional trading associations.

A decline in the influence of nation-states and a rise in the influence of transnational ties—economic, social, and political.

Less mass employment, with more specialization and production by small firms.

Less stable employment, with more temporary work and frequent job changes.

Ever greater labor skill requirements, with continual changes in demand for human capital, and a concomitant reduction in demand for unskilled and low-skilled physical labor.

Greater geographic mobility of workers, including mobility across national borders.

More workers who are essentially entrepreneurs selling their talents in the marketplace.

Household income from more varied sources, combinations of "regular" employment, temporary employment, entrepreneurial activity, and asset earnings. Just as many impoverished households today "patch" income from multiple sources to survive, the middle class will be more likely to do so tomorrow.

Work life not as rigidly confined by location, daily hours, or period in the life-span. There will be more variation, more gradualism, and more transitions in and out of the labor market over the life cycle.

Individuals and households in more divergent circumstances with many divergent "needs," as opposed to mass needs defined by mass labor markets.

People living longer, and more people who are healthy and capable in their older years.

Retirement largely redefined as a less definite stage in the life cycle, with greater emphasis on social engagement and economic productivity during the older years. The elderly will engage in a mix of productive activities—including paid labor, entrepreneurship, caretaking of family members, community volunteering, and civic involvement—in addition to retirement leisure.

SOCIAL POLICY IN THE TWENTY-FIRST CENTURY: THREE MAJOR GOALS

Social policy in the twenty-first century is likely to have three major goals, equally emphasized:

Social protection goals to buffer hardship and promote social stability. This has been the primary (almost exclusive) theme of twentieth-century welfare states, and it should certainly be retained in the twenty-first century. The focus is on standard of living, coverage and adequacy, and minimum protections at the bottom. Social welfare is defined in terms of income and consumption.

Development goals. Domestic policy should also promote the economic and social development of families and households, empowering citizens and promoting active participation in work, family and community life, and civic affairs. At the household level, development goals are likely to become as important as social protection goals in social policy.

Macroeconomic goals. As is now apparent to almost everyone, it is insufficient to think merely in terms of households in social security policy. Policy makers must simultaneously consider the macroeconomic goals of savings and investment, a strong and stable currency, development of securities markets, and economic growth.

In a word, twenty-first century social policy is very likely to move beyond the simplistic idea of consumption support, aiming for greater development of households, communities, and societies as a whole.

THE CONTINUING SHIFT TOWARD ASSET-BASED POLICY

The pressure of aging populations on PAYG social insurance systems will be the primary engine for policy change in the years ahead. The change will be away from unfunded social insurance and toward funded systems, very likely in the form of individual accounts, as is already occurring in many nations. This is not so much a matter of political ideology, but of arithmetic. In the United States, for example, it will make little difference in 2020 whether the Radical Right or the Progressive Left controls the federal government; Social Security policy will have changed dramatically because the current benefit structure is not sustainable unless payroll tax rates rise to 30 or 40 percent or higher (Bipartisan Commission, 1994), which almost no one would suggest is economically desirable or politically feasible. Thus, as defined benefit social insurance systems come under increasing fiscal pressure, they will be augmented and in some cases largely replaced by defined contribution systems. By the middle of the twenty-first century, I would anticipate that social insurance will no longer be the dominant pillar in social security policy in most countries; it will have been replaced by asset accounts.

Individual accounts will better fit the emerging information age economy, enabling people to navigate more individualized courses in the more specialized and fluid labor markets that are likely to characterize the twenty-first century. Workers will carry fully portable benefits with them in and out of the labor market, from employer to employer, even across national boundaries. In this manner, asset accounts will become a tool not merely for social security, but also for social and economic development of individuals and families. The twentieth century distinction between social and economic policy will largely disappear.

This policy shift is consistent with Thomas Jefferson's views on property owning and democracy in the United States, and it is also consistent with Lee Kuan Yew's goal of making Singaporeans home owners so they will be more strongly committed to the nation. In many different countries and cultures, considerable empirical research documents positive economic, personal, social, and civic effects of asset holding. The effects of asset holding may include longer time horizons, greater work effort, more involvement in the community, increased political participation, a more stable family life, and better economic and social outcomes for children (Sherraden, 1991; Page-Adams and Sherraden, 1996). In other words, the value of assets is probably far greater than their value as a storehouse for future consumption.

At the macroeconomic level, markets do not always get everything right, and one area where markets require assistance from public policy is in generating savings. It is clear from examples such as Singapore and Chile that social security policy based on asset accumulation can make enormous contributions to rates of internal savings and economic growth. In the twenty-first century, we will not think exclusively in terms of social protections at the expense of economic growth. We will instead think of social protections *and* economic growth (World Bank, 1994).

CONCERNS IN ASSET-BASED SOCIAL POLICY

As indicated above, there will in all likelihood be a shift toward asset-based policy in the next century, and in fact it is already occurring. But the vision of asset-based policy that I have presented above is highly idealized. No policy system is perfect, and there is a possibility of major deviations from what I have suggested. Indeed, there are a number of reasons to be wary of the shift to asset accounts. Permit me to mention three major concerns.

Coverage and Adequacy

A key issue is whether progressive principles are possible in a defined contribution system. How can we ensure principles of inclusion, solidarity, and progressivity in a system of social security based on asset accumulation? The shift to asset-based policy could occur but leave many people behind, excluded from social protections. In this regard, asset accounts could be even more regressive than social insurance. Indeed, this outcome is likely in many of the reforms that are now taking place in Latin America. If the shift to asset accounts is to be successful in the long run, extraordinary efforts must be made to bring everyone into the primary asset-based policy system. This will require as a first step the creation of accounts for all citizens at the youngest possible age, preferably at birth. Once such accounts are in place, a wide range of creative funding strategies can be developed to build the assets of the poor. This would be funding "up front" in a savings system so that people can invest in themselves and become more secure and more productive.

Protection of Funds

Another major concern is the protection of funds that individuals have saved and invested. For most countries, the best strategy will be to use financial markets for investments, as in the Chilean model and 401(k)s in the United States. The simple reason is that, unfortunately, there are few governments in the world that are capable of managing tens or hundreds of billions of dollars over the long term without depleting the resources in one way or another. On the other hand, care must also be taken to ensure the protection of funds in private security markets, particularly where these markets may not be fully developed. The infusion of funds from an asset-based social security system can be a major vehicle for building financial markets in developing nations, but until those markets are reliable and efficient, the government must play a major oversight role.

Implications for Freedom and Democracy

Because Singapore and Chile are the world's most extensive examples of asset-based policy, a question naturally arises about the role of authoritarianism in a defined contribution social security system. Some have argued that only in an authoritarian regime is it possible to shift to mandatory savings on a large scale (see chapter 5). This is a valid concern, but it applies primarily to implementation. Big policy changes of any kind are more challenging in a democracy—indeed this is the strength of democracy, and we would not want, under any circumstances, to sacrifice this strength for the expedience of authoritarianism. However, the example of Australia (chapter 2) indicates that transformational policy changes toward mandatory savings are indeed possible in a democracy. Looking ahead, we will very likely see similar changes in many of the major democracies of Western Europe and North America over the next two or three decades.

Regarding the issue of compulsory savings, mandatory contributions in social security have a well-established history in all the major democracies in the world. The only difference in an asset-based system would be that the payments go into a defined contribution rather than a defined benefit system. Once implemented, a defined contribution social security system is entirely consistent with democratic principles, with one major caveat: so long as all citizens have adequate assets in their accounts to meet their social development and security goals. If this condition is met, individual accounts are in many respects the most democratic of all policy mechanisms; they give greater individual control and enable families to shape their own social development and security decisions.

CONCLUSION

It has often been said that a social security system must fit the historical, cultural, social, political, and economic conditions in a particular country at a particular moment in history. As conditions change, system characteristics must change as well. Clearly the welfare states are in the midst of a major transition in social policy. The change is in many respects inevitable. Industrial era social security systems, based on stable mass employment, do not fit the characteristics of labor markets that are emerging in the information economy. The source of change is thus more economic than political or ideological, and the outcome is likely to be a slow form of the "radical surgery" that Senator Breaux mentioned in the foreword: a greater emphasis on "privatized" social security in the form of individual asset accounts. This will not happen all at once, but in erratic steps over several decades.

What does this mean for those of us who have progressive values? We should not delude ourselves: very real dangers lie ahead. If social security policy shifts to asset accounts, it is quite possible, even likely, that the poor will be hurt more than they are helped by these changes in the welfare states. It will be easy, and politically expedient, to shift to asset accounts and leave the poor behind with an inferior and politically vulnerable means-tested system. Other policy options, such as greater reliance on community groups or occupational protections, could also leave the poor behind. This would be a tragic mistake.

However, it need not occur. If we are creative, engaged, and active, we can define and promote policies that are in the best interests of all members of society. If we do move toward asset accounts, it is imperative that everyone have an account and that accounts are adequately funded to promote the security and development of everyone. This is not merely a matter of social justice, but of social and economic development of the nation as a whole. Increasingly, it will be important to develop to the fullest possible extent the talents and skills of all members of society. Nations that fail to do so will not compete well in the global economy. Thus, active progressive principles are required for inclusion of the entire population in social development and economic growth. To a considerable extent, we have to learn how to do this, but as we proceed we can keep in mind one of the most important points in this book, offered by Midgley in the introduction, which is that *progressive principles are possible in forms other than social insurance.* This simple observation is the key to intellectual and practical leadership in grappling with the inevitable changes in social security policy in the decades ahead.

NOTE

This chapter borrows in part from the author's presentation, "Social security in the twenty-first century," introductory paper at the International Symposium on Social Security in the Twenty-First Century, Mexico City, 12–14 March 1996.

REFERENCES

Bipartisan Commission on Entitlement and Tax Reform (1994) *Interim report to the President.* Washington, D.C.: U.S. Government Printing Office.

Glennerster, Howard and James Midgley (1991) *The Radical Right and the welfare state: An international assessment.* London: Harvester Wheatsheaf.

Marshall, T. H. (1964) *Class, citizenship, and social development.* Garden City, N.Y.: Doubleday.

Marx, Karl [1867] (1967) *Capital: A critique of political economy.* New York: International Publishers.

Midgley, James (1996) Toward a developmental model of social policy: Relevance of the Third World experience, *Journal of Sociology and Social Welfare* (23): 59–74.

Page-Adams, Deborah and Michael Sherraden (1996) *What we know about effects of asset holding: Implications for policy and research.* Working paper no. 96–1. St. Louis: Center for Social Development, Washington University.

Ruiz Durán, Clemente, ed. (forthcoming) *Proceedings of the international symposium on social security in the twenty-first century.* Mexico City: National University of Mexico.

Sherraden, Michael (1991) *Assets and the poor: A new American welfare policy.* Armonk, N.Y.: M. E. Sharpe.

The World Bank (1994) *Averting the old age crisis.* Washington, D.C.: The World Bank.

Index

Aboriginal Australians, mortality rates of, 30

Actuarially based, accumulated funds, 9

Administration: Australian program, 28; British pensions, 100, 101; Chilean social security, 78–80, 85–86; Hong Kong social assistance, 68, 126–27; Kenyan social security, 116; provident funds, 36; Singapore provident fund, 38, 126; U.S. Social Security, 12–13

Africa, social security coverage rates in, 106

Age Pension, in Australia, 18–19, 22–24, 26, 27, 28, 29

Agrarian labor, in Kenya, 112

Agrarian subsistence economy, 105, 106

Annuity, superannuation taken as, 124

Argentina, defined contribution system in, 87–88, 123

Asian countries: disdain for welfare state, 64; savings rates in, 54; social security coverage rates, 106

Asset-based policy: future trends, 132, 135–38; in Singapore, 33, 34, 37, 125; in Western welfare states, 54–55

Asset holding, well-being effects of, 50, 55, 136

Assets test: Australia, 23, 28, 29; Hong Kong, 66

Australia: contributory retirement programs, 17, 24–27, 124; demography, 18–19, 22; private occupational pensions in, 14, 17, 24, 124–25; social assistance in, 14, 17–31, 124–25

Authoritarian governments: in Chile, 76, 77–78, 86–87, 127, 137; in Singapore, 53, 125–26, 137

Baby boomers, retiring, 9–10

Basic state pension, in Britain, 97–98, 99

Benefits: entitlement to, 4; portability of, 38, 100, 127, 135–36

Beveridge Report, 4–5, 94, 96

Birth rate, in U.S., 9–10

Bonus payment, Chilean pension funds and, 85

Britain, 3, 92; Australian links to, 18; Beveridge Report, 4–5, 94, 96; evolution of social security system in, 4–5, 61, 93–96; market system in, 76; National Pension Savings Scheme, 100–101, 102; pension reform in, 91–103, 127–28; private occupational pensions in, 15, 95–103, 123; privatization of social security in, 15, 88, 95–103, 123, 127–28; social security reforms in, 15, 62, 88, 95–103, 123, 127–28; welfare institutions in, 37, 62

British colonies: Hong Kong, 62–63, 70, 71; provident funds in, 35, 36, 37, 40

Canada, social welfare spending in, 62

Capital: Australian need for, 29; Chilean markets, 79, 80, 84

Capital accumulation: Singapore, 34, 37, 125; social security effects on, 11–12

Capital availability, in Australia, 25

Capital flight, 11

Capitalized savings, provident funds providing, 5

Carer pensions, in Australia, 20

Casual work, 31, 112

Catastrophic protection, Singapore provident fund used for, 39, 43

Central Provident Fund of Singapore, 33–55, 125–26

Charitable activities, 3

Child benefit program, in Britain, 93

Chile: privatization of social security in, 15, 75–89, 123, 126; provident fund and, 5, 127

China. See People's Republic of China

Churches, Kenyan social security and, 113

Civil servants: in Britain, 96; in Chile, 77; in Hong Kong, 69; indigenous social security and, 110; in Kenya, 112, 115

Colombia, defined contribution system in, 87–88, 123

Commercially managed pension plans, in Britain, 95

Commercial sector, social policy and, 123

Commissions, Chilean pension funds and, 80, 83

Community, indigenous social security and, 109, 112, 115, 128

Company Welfarism through Employers' Contributions, in Singapore, 42

Comprehensive Social Security Assistance Scheme, in Hong Kong, 64–65

Compulsory contributions: Australian system, 14, 26, 124; British private pensions, 99, 102, 127; Chilean system, 79, 80, 81, 82; Singaporean system, 14, 33–55, 125–26; U.S. Social Security, 2–3

Compulsory saving, provident fund enforcing, 5

Compulsory superannuation, 26

Constitutional struggle, U.S. Social Security and, 7

Consumption: in Singapore, 50, 51; Western welfare states, 55, 129, 130

Consumption expenditure, Social Security as, 10

Contribution rates, Singapore provident fund, 39

Contributory occupational superannuation, 24–27

Contributory systems: Australia, 17, 24–27, 124; Hong Kong, 68–71; Kenya, 115

Cooperative associations, 112, 113

Corporate pensions funds, in Hong Kong, 69

Corporate provision of services and protections, 122

Costs: Australian program, 28; British pensions, 98, 101; Chilean social security, 84, 85–86; fiscal pressures created by rising, 91, 130, 131

Cultural beliefs, charitable activities mandated by, 3

Cultural characteristics, affecting savings behavior, 54

Currency depreciation, provident fund effects on, 36

Death, employment caused, 5, 6
Death benefits: Britain, 95; Chilean so-
cial security, 85; Kenyan welfare as-
sociations, 113; Singapore provident
fund, 39, 40, 42; U.S. Social Secu-
rity, 2, 6
Defined benefit systems, 123–24, 132
Defined contribution principles, 123–
24
Defined contribution systems, 135–38;
Britain, 88, 127–28; protection of
funds, 137; provident funds and, 35,
38; Singapore provident fund, 38
Demogrant schemes, 122; in Hong
Kong, 5, 14–15, 61–72, 126–27
Demographic changes, 124, 130, 134
Demographic trends, 124, 130, 134;
Australian, 18–19, 22; U.S., 9–10
Dependence on government, 7
Dependents of disabled persons, U.S.
Social Security benefits for, 6
Dependents' Protection, Singapore
provident fund used for, 46
Dependent survivors: British benefits,
94; U.S. Social Security benefits for,
2, 3, 5, 6
Depression, Great, 1–2
Developing countries: indigenous sys-
tems in, 15, 105–119; provident
funds in, 5, 36
Dialysis services, 6
Disability benefits, 4; Australia, 17, 20;
Britain, 93, 94; Chile, 85; Hong
Kong, 64, 65, 66; Singapore, 39, 40,
42; United States, 2, 3, 6, 7
Divorce, in the United States, 9

Early retirement, 9, 31
Earnings, linking old-age income to,
26
East Asia, savings rates in, 54
Economic change: information revolution and, 133–34; Kenya and, 112;
processes of, 87
Economic development, 135; Australia,
29; Chile, 80; Third World, 105–6
Economic effects, of Singapore provident fund, 50

Economic growth, 138; Australia, 21;
Chile, 79, 84; Hong Kong, 63–64, 67;
Kenya, 112; Singapore, 34, 37, 44;
social security effects on, 11; United
States, 10–12
Economic impact, of Chilean social security, 84–86
Economic need, concept of, 26
Economic policies: in Chile, 83; in Singapore, 33–34
Economic rationalism, 21
Economic trends, in the United States,
9
Education: in Kenya, 113; Singapore
provident fund used for, 38, 42, 44,
46, 49, 54
Efficiency: Australian system, 28; Chilean social security, 81–82; provident
funds, 37; U.S. system, 12–13
Eligibility, 4; Australian assistance, 17,
20, 21, 23, 28, 29, 30–31; British social allowances, 93, 94; Chilean social security, 77, 80; Hong Kong
system, 14, 66, 67; noncontributory
social allowances, 61
Elizabethan Poor Law of 1601 (Britain), 4
Employee contributions: British pensions, 95, 97, 99, 102; Chilean social
security, 78, 79, 80, 82; Hong Kong
social insurance, 70; provident
funds, 35, 38, 39; Singapore provident fund, 38, 39; U.S. Social Security, 2
Employees. See Workers
Employer-based superannuation
schemes, in Australia, 24–27
Employer contributions: British occupational pensions, 97, 99–100, 102;
Chilean social security, 78; Hong
Kong social insurance, 70; Kenyan
system, 111; provident funds, 35, 38,
39, 42; Singapore provident fund,
38, 39, 42; U.S. Social Security, 2
Employer liability approach, 5
Employment: future trends, 133, 134,
135; injury or death caused by, 5, 6;
U.S. levels, 9

Entrepreneurial activity, 134
Equity: Australian system, 29, 30; British occupational pensions, 98; Kenyan system, 112, 115; Singapore provident fund, 51, 54; Third World social security, 106; welfare states, 130, 131
European countries: demogrant schemes, 5; labor skill, 11; privatizing social security in, 88; social security in, 1
Expenditures: Australian assistance, 22; Chilean social security, 84–85

Families, 5; asset transfers in, 50, 53, 54, 111; British social allowances, 93; Chilean allowances program, 77; Chinese, 68; mutual help relations, 106, 108, 109, 110, 112, 113, 118, 128; social policy and, 123. *See also* Sole parenthood
Family formation, Singapore provident fund effects on, 50, 52–53
Family income, Australian social assistance and, 26–27
Family responsibility, provident funds based on, 38
Family structure, in United States, 9
Female labor force participation: Australia, 19, 21, 23, 27; Singapore, 50, 53; United States, 7, 9
Females: Australian pension eligibility, 20, 27, 30; British pensions, 97; Chilean pensions, 83; U.S. coverage rates, 7
Finance Act of 1956 (Britain), 97
Fiscal pressures, 91, 130, 131
Fiscal viability, of U.S. Social Security, 8–10
Fiscal welfare system, in Britain, 93
Foreign investment: Chilean pension funds, 84; in China, 11
France: demogrant system, 61; history of relief for poor in, 4; social security reforms, 131
Friends: indigenous social security and, 109, 110, 118; social policy and, 123

Funded accounts, Singapore provident fund and, 38
Funded approach, 9, 124
Funeral benefit, 6

Geographic mobility of workers, 134
Geographical spaces, indigenous social security and, 110
Germany: history of social insurance in, 4, 61; social security reforms, 131
Global economy, 130, 134
Government: Britain, 95; Chile, 76, 77–78, 82, 86–87, 127, 137; continuum of responsibility, 122; dependence on, 7; growth of, 12; Latin American countries, 87–88; Singapore, 53, 137; social policy and, 123; subsidiarity principle, 115
Government securities, Singapore provident fund invested in, 38
Government services, demands for, 12
Great Depression, 1–2
Gross domestic product (Singapore), savings rate as percent of, 54
Gross domestic product (U.S.), Social Security and Medicare as percentage of, 7

Harambee (cooperative) movement, 113
Health care: Australian system, 24, 28; Singapore provident fund used for, 38, 39, 40, 42, 44, 46, 48, 50; U.S. Social Security provisions for, 6
Health insurance: Australia, 24; U.S. elderly, 6
Home ownership: Australian pensioners, 23, 28; Singapore provident fund used for, 34, 38, 39, 40, 41, 43, 46, 48, 52
Hong Kong: demogrant scheme in, 5, 14–15, 61–72, 126–27
Housing: Australian assistance, 22–23; Hong Kong assistance, 64; provident funds used for, 34, 35

Illness benefits, 4, 17, 20; Britain, 94; Kenyan welfare associations, 113

Immigrant workers: Australia, 18, 31;
    indigenous social security and, 110
Inclusion principles, 136
Income: future trends, 134; Singapore,
    44; women's in Australia, 27
Income replacement, principle of, 26
Income Tax Act of 1952 (Britain), 97
Income test, 4; Australian system, 28,
    29; British social allowances, 93;
    Hong Kong social assistance, 66
India, social assistance retirement pen-
    sions in, 31
Indigenous social security: characteris-
    tics of, 107–11; integrating with stat-
    utory schemes, 108, 109, 111–19; in
    Kenya, 15, 105, 111–19, 128; rele-
    vance to industrial nations, 117–19
Individual accounts, Singapore provi-
    dent fund and, 38
Industrial countries, welfare pluralism
    in, 15
Industrialism, assumptions about, 129
Inflation: Australia, 25; Kenya, 113; so-
    cial security effects on, 12; United
    States, 9
Informal economy, in Kenya, 115
Information revolution, 132–34
Injury, employment caused, 5, 6
Insurance method of funding, 2–3
Insurance schemes, in Britain, 93, 94
Intergenerational asset transfers, 50,
    53, 54, 111
Intergenerational equity, 10
Intergenerational welfare transfer, 129
International donor community, Kenya
    and, 114
International Social Security Adminis-
    tration, Committee on Provident
    Funds, 36
Investments: British National Pension
    Savings Scheme, 101; British occupa-
    tional pensions, 97; Chilean pension
    funds, 83, 84; Chilean social secu-
    rity, 80; Hong Kong, 63; Singapore
    provident fund, 38, 39, 41, 42, 43,
    44, 46, 48, 50; well-being effects, 55
Investment companies, managing Brit-
    ish pensions plans, 95

Investment decisions, labor costs af-
    fecting, 11

Japan, social insurance system in, 130
Job creation, Social Security payroll
    tax effects on, 10–11
Job placement, for disabled recipients,
    6
Job search, 22
Johnson administration, introduction
    of Medicare by, 6

Kenya, indigenous system in, 15, 105,
    111–19, 128
Kinship-based relations of mutual
    help, 106, 108, 109, 110, 112, 113,
    118, 128

Labor costs, 10–11
Labor markets: Australian trends, 19,
    21; distortion of, 10; future trends,
    133, 134, 135
Labor-saving technologies, 10–11
Labor skill, 11, 134
Latin American countries, 1; privatiz-
    ing social security in, 87–88, 123,
    127; social security coverage rates,
    106; unionized labor force and, 130
Left. See Political left
Life annuity, Chilean social security,
    80
Life cycle, 134
Life expectancy: Australia, 18–19;
    United States, 10
Life insurance, Singapore provident
    fund coverage, 42, 44
Living standards, community expecta-
    tions about, 27
Lobbying, by Australian pensioners, 29
Low-wage employment, 31
Lump-sum payment: provident funds,
    37, 40, 46, 50; Singapore provident
    fund, 40, 46, 50; superannuation
    taken as, 124

Macroeconomic adjustments, Singa-
    pore provident fund used for, 39
Macroeconomic goals, 135

Males: Australian pension eligibility, 20, 30; British pensions, 97; Chilean benefits, 83; U.S. coverage rates, 7

Male labor force participation: Australia, 19, 20; United States, 7, 9

Managerial efficiency, 12–13

Market system, in Chile, 76–77

Married couples, Australian pensions and, 22, 23

Maternity benefits, in Britain, 94

Means test, 4; Australia, 17, 18–19, 23, 28, 29; Britain, 93, 94; Hong Kong, 64, 66

Medical care. See Health care

Medicare, 6

Medisave, 40, 42, 44, 46, 48

Medishield, 43, 46

Mexico, defined contribution system in, 123

Middle class, welfare state spending on, 130, 131

Migrant workers: Australia, 18, 31; Singapore, 40

Migration, indigenous social security and, 110

Migration flows, 18, 31

Military pensions: Australia, 20, 22; Chile, 83–84; Kenya, 112

Modernization, influence on Third World, 106

Mortgages, reverse, 50

Multilayered functional perspective, 109

Mutual aid societies, 4

National boundary problems, 130

National Hospital Insurance Fund, in Kenya, 112

National Insurance Act of 1946 (Britain), 94–95, 96

National Pension Savings Scheme, British proposal for, 100–101, 102

National Social Security Fund, in Kenya, 112

Nation-states, decline in influence of, 134

Neighborhood, indigenous social security and, 109, 118

Neoclassical theory, 55

Neo-Marxist theme, 122

New Deal, 7, 117

Noncash benefits, for Australian pensioners, 22, 24, 29

Noncontributory pensions: Australia, 17–31; Hong Kong, 5, 14–15, 61–72, 126

Nongovernmental organizations, in Kenya, 113–14, 128

Nonprofit sector, social policy and, 123

Nonprofit services and provisions, 122

Nonresidential property investments, Singapore provident fund used for, 42, 46, 48

Occupational pensions. See Private occupational pensions

Occupational provision of services and protections, 122

Occupational welfare, 42

Old-age income, linking to earnings, 26

Old Age Pensions Act of 1908 (Britain), 94

Old-age retirement, 4; Australia, 18–19, 22–24, 26, 27, 28, 29, 125; Britain, 94; Hong Kong, 65–69; United States, 2, 3, 5, 6–7

Older workers, labor force participation of, 21–22

Pacific Islands, provident fund development in, 35, 37

Partitioned accounts, Singapore provident fund and, 38

Part-time workers, 31, 99

Patron-client interactions, indigenous social security and, 109, 110

Pay-as-you-go system, 9, 91, 124, 130

Payment errors, 13

Pension assets, ownership of, 100

Pension fund management corporations, in Chile, 80

Pension reform, in Britain, 91–103, 127–28

People's Republic of China: administration of Hong Kong by, 63, 70–71, 126; foreign investment in, 11

Personal pension plans, in Britain, 95–97

Peru, defined contribution system in, 87–88, 123

Pinochet regime, 76–77, 83

Political impact, of Chilean social security, 86–87

Political left: British pension reforms and, 98; social policy and, 122

Political right: British occupational pensions and, 98; challenge to state-sponsored welfare, 62, 117; social policy and, 122, 131; U.S. Social Security issues, 2, 8

Politicians, addressing Social Security issues, 2

Politics: Australian, 19, 29; British, 98; Chilean, 76; Singaporean, 53; U.S., 2, 8, 88, 131

Poor, charity for, 3–4

Poor Law Reform Act of 1834 (Britain), 96

Portability of benefits, 38, 100, 127, 135–36

Poverty: Australia, 20, 27, 30; Britain, 96; Chile, 84; Hong Kong, 15, 69; Kenya, 112, 114, 116; United States, 2, 7

Private charity, 122

Private occupational pensions, 92, 93; in Australia, 14, 17, 124–25; in Britain, 15, 95–103, 123

Privatization of social security, 122, 135–38; Argentina, 88, 123; Britain, 88, 127–28; Chile, 15, 75–89, 123, 126

Progressivity principles, 136

Provident funds, 122; British colonies, 35, 36, 37, 40; Chile, 5, 127; Hong Kong, 69; origin and development of, 35–37; Singapore, 14, 33–55, 123, 125–26

Psychological effects, of asset holding, 50, 136

Public assistance, in Hong Kong, 64–65, 126. See also Social assistance

Public housing, Singapore provident fund used for, 40, 46, 48

Public sector, growth of, 12

Public support: Australian system, 14, 22, 28, 29–30; Hong Kong social insurance, 69, 70, 71; U.S. Social Security, 88

Public views: Chilean social security, 81–82; future of social security, 91–92; Singapore provident fund, 49–51

Recession: in Chile, 84; in the United States, 9

Redistribution of resources, 110, 123–24

Redistributive principles, 27, 123–24

Rehabilitation, 6, 22

Religious beliefs, charitable activities mandated by, 3

Resources: availability of, 108; redistribution of, 110, 123–24

Retirement: Chilean social security, 77, 78; early, 9, 31; provident funds used for, 35, 39, 48; as reward, 129; Singapore provident fund benefits, 39, 48. See also Old-age retirement

Retraining, 22

Right. See Political right

Roosevelt administration, New Deal and, 7

Rotating savings and credit associations, 111, 112, 113

Rural-urban linkages, indigenous social security and, 110

Savings: Asian countries, 54; Australia, 25, 29; Britain, 93, 99, 127; Chile, 79, 80, 84; compulsory, 5, 33–55, 79, 127; cultural characteristics affecting, 54; provident funds, 5, 33–55; Singapore, 33–55; social security effects on, 11–12; well-being effects of having, 55

Self-employment: Britain, 99; Kenya, 112, 115; Singapore, 39, 40, 54; United States, 2, 9

Self-help groups, Kenyan social security and, 111, 113, 115–16

Shares Top-Up, Singapore provident
    fund used for, 43, 44, 46, 48, 50, 54
Sickness benefits. *See* Illness benefits
Singapore, provident fund approach
    in, 14, 33–55, 123, 125–26
Social allowances, 122; Britain, 93;
    Chile, 77, 27; Hong Kong, 5, 61–72,
    126–127. *See also* Demogrant
    schemes
Social assistance, 61, 122; advantages
    of, 27–31; alternative to, 4; Australia,
    14, 17–31, 124–25; Britain, 3, 93; dis-
    advantages of, 27–31; Hong Kong,
    64–65, 126; percentage of Western
    government budgets devoted to, 54–
    55; United States, 3; worldwide
    trends in, 132
Social assistance model, 26
Social change: indigenous social secu-
    rity relations, 111; information revo-
    lution and, 133–34; Kenya, 112
Social development, 138
Social impact: of asset holding, 50, 136;
    Chilean social security, 86; Singa-
    pore provident fund, 37, 44–50, 52–
    53
Social insurance, 4, 61, 122; assump-
    tions about industrialism, 129; Hong
    Kong, 68–71; percentage of Western
    government budgets devoted to, 54–
    55
Socialism, 122
Social policy: actors in, 123; asset-
    based, 34, 37, 54–55, 125, 132, 135–
    38; Australia, 124–25; Britain, 97–98;
    Chile, 127; comprehensive changes
    in, 124; Hong Kong, 66–67, 126; in-
    digenous social security institutions,
    107; Kenya, 114–16, 128; Singapore,
    33–34, 35, 37, 38, 42, 43–49, 125–26;
    twentieth century, 128–29; twenty-
    first century, 134–35; welfare states,
    54–55, 129–30; worldwide trends in,
    132
Social provision of goods and services,
    122
Social reform, Australian agenda for,
    20–21

Social relationships, indigenous social
    security and, 106, 108, 109–11, 112,
    113, 118
Social security: conditions of, 108–9;
    Europe, 1; future of, 2, 8, 91–92,
    121–39; global expansion of, 1; his-
    tory of, 1, 3–5; mechanisms of, 108,
    109–10; multiple pillars, 109, 121,
    132; partnerships in, 122–23; savings
    effects, 11–12; twenty-first century,
    121–39; welfare state linkages, 5. *See
    also specific countries*
Social Security, U.S.: expenditures for,
    7; features of, 2–7; fiscal viability of,
    8–10; future of, 2, 8, 131; history of,
    1; number of recipients, 6; problems
    of, 7–13
Social Security Act of 1935, U.S., 5
Social Security Allowance Scheme, in
    Hong Kong, 65–69
Social security deficit, in Chile, 85
Social security funding: Australia, 20;
    Britain, 99–100; Chile, 78–80;
    funded approach, 9, 124; Hong
    Kong, 65, 68, 70; non -contributory
    social allowances, 61; pay-as-you-go,
    9, 91, 124, 130; United States, 2–3, 8–
    10
Social security policy, options in, 121–
    24
Social security reforms, 117; Australia,
    20–21, 24–25; Britain, 62, 91–103,
    127–28; Chile, 75–89; fiscal crises
    and, 131; Hong Kong, 68–71, 126;
    United States, 3, 88
Social solidarity principle, 86
Social welfare: commercial providers
    of, 118; in Hong Kong, 64; in
    Kenya, 114
Social welfare associations, 112, 113
Society accounts, 100
Sole parenthood: Australian assistance,
    17, 20; Hong Kong assistance, 65
Solidarity principles, 123–24, 136
South Africa, social assistance retire-
    ment pensions in, 31
Southeast Asia, savings rates in, 54

Special Discounted Shares. *See* Shares Top-Up
Spouse, Australian pension eligibility and, 23
Standard of living, U.S., 9
State Earnings-Related Pensions Scheme, in Britain, 95
State responsibility, continuum of, 122
Statutory schemes, integrating with indigenous systems, 108, 109, 111–19
Stigma, for social assistance recipients, 28–29, 94, 125
Structural adjustment programs, in Kenya, 113
Subsidiarity principle, 114–15
Superannuation: Australia, 17, 24–27, 29, 123, 124–25; Britain, 95
Superannuation Guarantee Charge, 17, 26–27
Survivors. *See* Dependent survivors
Sweden: *folkpension*, 61–62, 72; social security reforms, 131

Targeting, in Australian system, 28
Taxation: Australian pensioners, 23–24, 29; British pension benefits, 97, 101; Hong Kong, 63, 65, 68; noncontributory social allowances funded by, 61; social policy and, 129
Tax benefits, of provident funds, 35, 38
Tax incentives, superannuation and, 124
Technologies: information, 133; laborsaving, 10–11
Thatcher administration, 95
Third World: agrarian economy in, 105, 106; Kenya, 105–19
Trade unions: Australia, 19, 25; Chile, 87; Kenya, 113, 115; Latin America, 130
Transnational ties, 134

Unemployment: Australia, 21–22; Britain, 98–99; Chile, 83; Hong Kong, 63; Kenya, 112, 115; United States, 9, 11
Unemployment benefits: Australia, 17,

20, 22; Britain, 95; social security assumptions about, 129
United States: commercial providers of social welfare services, 118; welfare institutions in, 62. *See also* Social Security, U.S.
Universal flat-rate benefits, in Britain, 94–95
Universal minimum pension, in Britain, 97
Universal schemes. *See* Demogrant schemes
Universal social allowances, in Britain, 93
Universal social protection, private sector and, 98

Veterans' pensions. *See* Military pensions
Village membership, indigenous social security and, 109
Vocational rehabilitation, for disabled recipients, 6
Voluntary sector: in industrial countries, 117–18; social policy and, 123
Voluntary social security organizations, 113, 115–16

Wages: Chile, 83; immigrant, 18
Wage demands: Australia, 25; social security effects on, 12
Wage employment: Kenya, 111; Third World, 106
Welfare: intergenerational transfer of, 129; occupational, 42
Welfare associations, in Kenya, 112, 113
Welfare consensus, postwar, 8
Welfare economics, 55
Welfare pluralism, 15, 117, 118
Welfare states, 4, 117, 122; Asian governments' disdain for, 64; asset-based policy in, 54–55; Australian, 26; British, 37; challenges to, 62; consumption and, 55, 129, 130; social policy in, 129–30; strain in, 131; U.S., 3

Well-being, saving and asset ownership
    effects on, 55
Western industrial countries: indige-
    nous social security's relevance to,
    117–19; voluntary sector in, 117–18
Widowhood pensions, in Australia, 20
Withdrawals, from Singapore provi-
    dent fund, 45–49
Women. *See* Females
Women's groups, Kenyan self-help,
    113

Work, changing patterns of, 31
Work incentives, social security effects
    on, 12
Workers: casual, 31, 112; future trends,
    133, 134, 135; geographic mobility
    of, 134; immigrant, 18, 31, 110; in-
    jury or death on the job, 5, 6; own-
    ership of pension assets, 100;
    part-time, 31; ratio of retired to ac-
    tive, 10, 22
Workmen's compensation, 5, 6

About the Contributors

FRANZ VON BENDA-BECKMANN is professor of law and rural development in Third World Countries at Wageningen Agricultural University. He has undertaken field work in Malawi, West Sumatra, and the Mouccas. He is the author of *Rechtpluralism in Malawi* (1970), *Property in Social Continuity* (1979), *Between Kinship and the State: Social Security Law in Developing Countries* (1988) (edited with others), and *Law as a Resource in Agrarian Struggles* (edited with M. van Velde). He has written many articles on legal pluralism, social security, and rural development issues and recently co-edited a special issue of the journal *Focaal* dealing with social security issues in developing nations.

SILVIA BORZUTSKY teaches political science at the University of Pittsburgh and Carnegie Mellon University. Her teaching and research concentrate on Latin American politics and social policy with emphasis on questions of democratization and neoliberal politics. She has published a number of articles on Chilean politics and social security. She has also written about health policies in Latin America.

FRANK FIELD is a Labour party member of Parliament for Birkenhead and serves as chairman of the British House of Commons Social Security Select Committee. Before entering the Commons in 1979, he was director of the Child Poverty Action Group and the Low Pay Unit. He is author of a number of books, most recently *Making Welfare Work* (1995).

HANS GSÄNGER is a senior research fellow at the German Development Institute in Berlin. He is an agricultural economist who has worked in development for about twenty-five years. He is particularly interested in agricultural and rural development and issues of social security and social policy. He has published a number of monographs and articles on these topics.

JAMES MIDGLEY is Dean of the School of Social Welfare at the University of California at Berkeley. From 1993 to 1996 he served as Associate Vice Chancellor for Research and Development at Louisiana State University, and from 1986 to 1993, he was Dean of the School of Social Work at LSU. Previously, he taught at the London School of Economics and the University of Cape Town. His many books include *Professional Imperialism: Social Work in the Third World* (1981); *The Social Dimensions of Development* (with Margaret Hardiman, 1982, revised 1989); *Social Security, Inequality and the Third World* (1984); *Community Participation, Social Development and the State* (with Anthony Hall, Margaret Hardiman, and Dhanpaul Narine, 1986); *Comparative Social Policy and the Third World* (with Stewart MacPherson, 1987); *Profiles in International Social Work* (with S. K. Khinduka and M. C. Hokenstad); and *Social Development: The Developmental Perspective in Social Welfare.* He has contributed to many leading social policy, social work, and development studies journals and has edited six special journal issues. He serves on the editorial boards of eight major journals.

MATTHEW OWEN is a senior equity analyst at the British financial firm, James Capel, in London. He previously worked as a research assistant to Frank Field and has co-authored *Private Pensions for All* (1993), *Europe Isn't Working* (1994), and *Beyond Punishment* (1994). He is a prospective parliamentary candidate for the Liberal Democratic party for which he also serves as a social affairs spokesperson.

LINDA S. ROSENMAN is professor of social policy and president of the Academic Board at the University of Queensland, Australia. She was previously head of the Department of Social Work and Social Policy at the University of Queensland. She has published widely on women, retirement, and economic support for women's caring. She is also actively involved in national social and tertiary educational policy development. Her recent publications include *The Price of Care* (1994), *Women's Work Patterns and the Impact upon Provision for Care* (1994), and *Retirement Policy, Retirement Incomes and Women* (1995).

MICHAEL SHERRADEN is Benjamin E. Youngdahl professor of social development at Washington University in St. Louis. He is also director of the Center for Social Development and chair of the doctoral program in social work. He has been active in the study of youth policy and has published *Community-based youth services in international perspective* (1992), which examines youth policy in five nations. He has contributed to national and community service in the United States by co-authoring *National Service: Social, economic, and military impacts* (with Donald Eberly, 1982) and *The moral equivalent of war? A study of non-military service in nine nations* (with Donald Eberly, 1990). In other work, Sherraden has studied and proposed asset-based alternatives in domestic policy; he is author of *Assets and the poor: A new American welfare policy* (1991).

K. L. TANG is an assistant professor of social work at the University of Northern British Columbia in Canada. He previously taught at Hong Kong Polytechnic University. He completed his doctoral studies at the University of California (Berkeley), where his dissertation was entitled *"Comparative Theories of Social Policy: A Historical Quantitative Study of Hong Kong"*. He has published several articles on comparative social policy, community development, and industrial social work.

ISBN 0-86569-245-9

EAN

9 780865 692459

90000>

HARDCOVER BAR CODE